Hansen's years of teaching international . . . senting theology through the acceptance . . . trying to resolve all the mysteries. We can all benefit from this fascinating and enlightening perspective.

—JOHN H. WALTON, Professor of Old Testament, Wheaton College

Truly a "eureka" book. If you've ever wondered how human free will and the will of God can coexist, or any number of apparent contradictions in the Bible can be resolved, here are your answers.

—DAVID WINTER, Hon. Canon of Christ Church, Oxford;
former Head of Religious Broadcasting, BBC

You'll love this book as it explores the wonder of a living God who exceeds all your expectations. *Paradox Lost* is a compelling and timely reminder that God transcends all the boxes we build for him.

—WAYNE JACOBSEN, author, *Finding Church*
and *He Loves Me*; coauthor, *The Shack*

With perception and depth, Hansen describes the paradoxes of the Christian faith and life. In doing so, he leads us to a deeper understanding of discipleship that includes humility and confidence and, above all, grace. An invaluable aid for our lifelong journey of following Jesus.

—PAUL E. PIERSON, Dean Emeritus, School of Intercultural
Studies, Fuller Theological Seminary

A highly stimulating, challenging, and well-balanced book. Hansen shows us that paradox reveals a holy, mysterious, and awesome God. I am looking forward to reading this book once more!

—KURT CHRISTENSEN, Professor of Theology,
Lutheran School of Theology, Aarhus, Denmark

Meet a very serious pastor, a world missionary, and a deeply searching scholar. You will never be ashamed of paradox again. And Jesus Christ himself, the Paradox par excellence, will be more revered than ever.

—FREDERICK DALE BRUNER, Wasson Professor Emeritus of Religion,
Whitworth University; author, *A Theology of the Holy Spirit*

Hansen tackles the often-mislabeled "contradictions" of Christianity with the mind of a scholar and the communication skills of a pastor who has interpreted these to people in all ages and stages of life. Hansen gives us a stimulating handbook for reflection, conversation, and ministry.

—Dr. Douglas J. Rumford, lead pastor, Trinity United Presbyterian Church; author, *SoulShaping: Taking Care of Your Spiritual Life*

This is a refreshing reminder that Christian life and witness is not so much about problem-solving as it is about living faithfully within the paradox and mystery of Christ. Rather than ending the journey of faith, this recognition invites exploration and true divine and self discovery.

—Thomas Alan Harvey, Academic Dean, Oxford Centre for Mission Studies

Rooted in Scripture at every turn, this profound book comes as a fresh wind, refreshing the mind and showing the way to the depth of knowing and being known that we all long for. Hansen's timely and prophetic book lifts our eyes to see how we more truly can be the people of God.

—James Starr, Professor of New Testament, Johannelund School of Theology

Hansen is so at home with ideas about biblical paradox that we hardly notice before this book has entered way down deep into our thoughts and feelings about God. Hansen's meditations supply many splendid images which steer us clear of simplistic thinking about the life of faith.

—Dustin Ellington, Lecturer in New Testament, Justo Mwale University (Zambia); Research Fellow, University of the Free State (Bloemfontein, South Africa)

Christianity is full of mysteries. They often look like paradoxes, whether in Christian life, biblical teaching, or core theology. Hansen helps us see how exploring those paradoxes is the way to a thriving, living faith.

—Gary Neal Hansen, Associate Professor of Church History, University of Dubuque Theological Seminary; author, *Kneeling with Giants*

The reality of God is too big and too complex for us to fully comprehend. Hansen understands that the solution is not to quit trying but rather to get comfortable with living in tension. As we embrace the mystery and paradox of God, we come to know him at deeper levels.

—Dr. Bob Logan, coach, consultant, and author, Logan Leadership, www.loganleadership.com

PARADOX
LOST

PARADOX
LOST

REDISCOVERING *the* MYSTERY *of* GOD

RICHARD P. HANSEN

ZONDERVAN

Paradox Lost
Copyright © 2016 by Richard P. Hansen

This title is also available as a Zondervan ebook.
Visit www.zondervan.com/ebooks.

Requests for information should be addressed to:
Zondervan, 3900 *Sparks Dr. SE, Grand Rapids, Michigan* 49546

Library of Congress Cataloging-in-Publication Data

Names: Hansen, Richard P., 1951- author.
Title: Paradox lost : rediscovering the mystery of God / Richard P. Hansen.
Description: Grand Rapids : Zondervan, 2016.
Identifiers: LCCN 2015043803 | ISBN 9780310518389 (softcover)
Subjects: LCSH: Spirituality — Christianity. | God (Christianity) — Knowableness. |
  Hidden God.
Classification: LCC BV4501.3 .H36255 2016 | DDC 230 — dc23 LC record available at
  http://lccn.loc.gov/2015043803

Cover design: *DualIndentity Design*
Cover photo: *Luke Mattson/Lightstock*
Interior illustrations: *Red Hansen, © 2015 by Zondervan*
Interior design: *Kait Lamphere*

Printed in the United States of America

16 17 18 19 20 21 22 23 24 25 26 /DHV/ 15 14 13 12 11 10 9 8 7 6 5 4 3 2 1

For Marilyn,
with all my love, always

CONTENTS

Acknowledgments. 11

PART 1: A STRANGE SORT OF COMFORT

1. A Strange Sort of Comfort 15
2. Fog 25
3. Newton's Apple 32

PART 2: SERIOUS PLAYFULNESS

4. Serious Playfulness 39
5. Try Harder! 45
6. New Frames 52
7. Terror and Truth on Flight 451 59
8. Pavlov's Dogs 65

PART 3: THE TUNING FORK

9. The Tuning Fork 73
10. 'Course He Isn't Safe . . . but He's Good 79
11. Now My Eyes See. 85
12. Who Chooses First? 92
13. Already . . . Not Yet 100

PART 4: THE TWO HANDLES

14. The Two Handles. 109
15. Eagles and Hippos 113
16. Treasure and Vessel. 124
17. All for a Letter 134
18. The Absurd 143

PART 5: THE SHELL

19. The Shell 155
20. If Not Certainty 164
21. Three Tensions. 171
22. Simplicity and Complexity. 179
23. Coastal Waters 186

Epilogue: The Duke Humfrey Library 195
Afterword: A Plea for Contrarian Preachers (and Listeners). . . 199
Appendix: Three Orders of Paradox 207
Notes. 209

ACKNOWLEDGMENTS

My interest in biblical paradox was sparked during a study fellowship graciously offered by Millikin University, Decatur, Illinois, in the early 1980s. I pursued this topic in a dissertation at Fuller Theological Seminary in the 1990s and am grateful to my supervisor, Ray Anderson, who offered a wealth of insight clarifying my germinating ideas. Doug Nason reviewed my dissertation with helpful suggestions and lasting encouragement. I wrote most of it while on sabbatical at Regent's Park College, Oxford University, and greatly appreciated both the warm welcome to our family and the interest in this project over the years shown by then principal Paul Fiddes. The concept of different genres or orders of paradox coalesced from many sources, both known and unknown; even though I cannot cite them all, I am thankful to them.

Many of these ideas were first shared with the church family of First Presbyterian Church, Visalia, California; they will always have a special place in my heart. Teaching systematic theology at the Ethiopian Graduate School of Theology (EGST) in Addis Ababa, Ethiopia, for four years offered me the rich opportunity to learn the importance of worldview and incorporate it into my thinking. To all my friends, colleagues, and, most of all, brothers and sisters in Christ in both Visalia and EGST, I am grateful for every kindness you offered me.

Wayne Jacobsen not only suggested this book's title but has encouraged my sporadic writing attempts over the past twenty-five years. Another partner on the journey who epitomizes an encouraging spirit to me is F. Dale Bruner, who commented on my dissertation years ago and then did the same with this manuscript. Others who read the entire manuscript and prodded me to improve in countless ways were Tom Elson, Nathan Hansen, Barbara Simpson, and James Starr. Dusty

Ellington and Kurt Christensen offered responses to specific chapters. All have my deepest thanks.

If paradox opens a door to the mystery of God, John Walton gave me the amazing gift of opening the door to Zondervan. I am grateful for the always-positive guidance and support of Madison Trammel throughout the process, especially during my wife's illness. Thanks to Madison and many others at Zondervan, this book became far more than I imagined it could be.

My children, Nathan (with Milli), Megan (with Joe), and Lauren, have all been encouragers of me and this book in ways small and large; they are all a profound blessing to me. The single factor that most powerfully shepherded this book from dream to reality is the tenacious, sacrificial love of my wife, Marilyn. Over the past forty-one years, she is the person who has consistently embodied God's grace in my life.

—*Rich Hansen, Thanksgiving Day 2015*

PART 1

A STRANGE SORT OF COMFORT

Chapter 1

A STRANGE SORT OF COMFORT

*The prudent thing in theology is never to go looking
for paradoxes but wait until you bump into one, as you
inevitably will.*
—George B. Hall, "D. M. Baillie: A Theology of Paradox"

C heryl's letter made my day.

Responding to a journal article I had written about preaching biblical paradox, she quickly moved from words of appreciation to the issues my article raised that were still vexing her. She wrote, "How can God still work his plan in my life when my free will keeps getting in the way and messing things up? How can he 'restore the years the locusts have eaten' when I am the one that invited those locusts to come and devour my life? How can he 'work all things together for good' when I keep getting in there with my free will and messing with his plans? On a larger scale, how can God work out his plan in the universe when men and women still have a free will to do their own thing apart from God's will?"

Good questions all! How human free will and God's sovereignty— two equally valid biblical notions that seem constantly at odds with each other—fit together has plagued the best minds Christianity has produced. Cheryl did what many over the centuries have done: she sought out other opinions. "I emailed several of my friends and asked for their input on this question. Along with some very good answers, I also received an answer of 'You think too much.' This answer bothered me a great deal, because in some respects I think the body of believers has been conditioned not to 'think too much.' We have been told (or it has been implied), 'Don't think too much about things that can't be explained.' 'Just take it by faith.' 'Don't ask too many questions; you'll make God look bad.' And so on."

I regularly encounter the same responses. Having pieces of truth scattered across the table without knowing where they fit in the puzzle can be threatening. It is doubly threatening when others tell us all the pieces *should* fit together (and that their puzzles have been assembled for years!). When you stop to consider, it is ludicrous to think that the God who gave humans the gift of intelligence could really be worried about looking bad when we ask questions. Yet earnest Christians often consider reason an enemy of faith. And if there is anything that gets reason riled up, it is paradox, defined by philosopher Gordon Graham as "anything which is intellectually objectionable but nevertheless unavoidable."[1]

Cheryl's wrestling with the paradoxical could have led her to conclude, "It's not worth the effort! Next time, I'll just swallow my questions." But she refused. "What I came away with from my struggle was not an attitude that says, 'Well, I'll never do that again' but rather a greater sense of how awesome God is and a strange sort of comfort stemming from the fact that I could not get my arms around this complicated concept."

It is Cheryl's "strange sort of comfort" that both intrigues and affirms me, for I have felt it as well. It is the strange comfort of knowing that our earthly journey resembles the switchbacks that climb Pike's Peak, however much we might wish it to be a straight interstate across Death Valley. A good deal of the perplexity, inconsistency, tension, and wonder of our lives, and the Christian faith itself, stems from paradox. Our very inability to get our arms around it releases us from our need to control it. As Cheryl says, we gain "a greater sense of how awesome God is."

"If I Had Not Struggled . . ."

Cheryl ended her letter to me with these words: "I finally was able to rest in the fact that 'there is a God and I am not he.' What peace I gained from that knowledge! However, if I had not struggled, I never would have come to know that peace and comfort, as well as a deeper knowledge of God."

Wrestling with Christian paradox, we reengage intellectually, and reexperience emotionally, that "there is a God and I am not he." We are spelunkers who, having spent many weary hours inching our way along a horizontal tunnel still close to the surface, suddenly happen upon a vertical shaft dropping straight into the dark, unknown depths. It looks foreboding. But if we risk our time and careful attention, climbing down step by cautious step, the deeper glories of the cave may be revealed in all their splendor. It was through her struggle to hang on to the paradoxical tensions of faith that Cheryl was led to the strange comfort that "there is a God and I am not he."

Living with such tensions is increasingly how I seem to spend my days. As I listen to people, I find I am not alone. While many inside and outside the Christian community yearn for a simple either/or world—the black hats (villains) and white hats (heroes) become easy to pick out as they ride toward us—real life often resides in both/and tensions. Such a nuanced view finds little support in a political culture that dumbs down complex issues to thirty-second sound bites, or in some churches that do the same with fill-in-the-blank sermon outlines.

During the height of the Cold War, Soviet scientist and human rights activist Aleksandr Solzhenitsyn wrote in *The Gulag Archipelago*, "If only there were evil people somewhere insidiously committing evil deeds, and it were necessary only to separate them from the rest of us and destroy them. But the line dividing good and evil cuts through the heart of every human being."[2] Our tendency to divide good and evil into mutually exclusive social or political polarities is rampant today. *New York Times* columnist David Brooks suggests we need leaders like Abraham Lincoln, who was a great president because he made room within himself for self-correcting tensions: a passionate advocate, but able to see his enemy's point of view; not afraid to wield power, yet aware of how much was beyond his control; extremely self-confident, but at the same time extremely humble.[3]

Dare we suggest that truth might sometimes reside *within* the tension created by opposing polarities? Dare we propose that the best policy choices may reside somewhere between Democrats and Republicans, left and right, MSNBC and Fox News? Have we lost our ability to live within (or even recognize) such tensions because we spend most of our time in echo chambers reverberating with the predispositions of people just like us?

In the Christian arena, can we admit tensions within our faith and risk being labeled unfaithful, unbiblical, humanistic, or secular or being told, "You think too much"? Is it possible to affirm right and wrong, moral absolutes, and biblical authority while also suggesting that truth sometimes resides between opposing absolutes? Ability to live within such tensions, polarities, and ambiguities, while not allowing them to paralyze our thinking or acting, is urgently needed today.

Tension in the Bible?

We tend to forget that living within such tensions is a major part of the biblical landscape. Think about some basic truths all Christians say we affirm:

- We see unseen things (2 Cor. 4:18).
- We find rest under a yoke (Matt. 11:28–30).
- We reign by serving (Mark 10:42–44).
- We are made great by becoming least (Luke 9:48).
- We are exalted by being humble (Matt. 23:12).
- We become wise by being fools for Christ's sake (1 Cor. 1:20–21).
- We gain strength by becoming weak (2 Cor. 12:10).
- We triumph through affliction (2 Cor. 12:7–9).
- We find victory by glorying in our infirmities (2 Cor. 12:5).
- We live by dying (John 12:24–25; 2 Cor. 4:10–11).

A. W. Tozer writes that a real Christian is an "odd number" because a believer "empties himself in order to be full; admits he is wrong so he can be declared right; goes down in order to get up; is strongest when he is weakest; richest when he is poorest; and happiest when he feels the worst. He dies so he can live; forsakes in order to have; gives away so he can keep; sees the invisible, hears the inaudible, and knows that which passeth knowledge."[4]

Reflecting on the brutal Serbian fighters who murdered, raped, and pillaged paths of destruction through his native Croatia, theologian Miroslav Volf narrates how he lives in tension: "My thought was pulled in two different directions by the blood of the innocent crying out to God and by the blood of God's Lamb offered for the guilty."[5] Volf wonders how he can remain loyal to the demand of the oppressed for justice yet at the same time uphold the forgiveness that God freely offers to the perpetrators of these horrendous crimes. He concludes that he is "divided between the God who delivers the needy and the God who abandons the Crucified, between the demand to bring about justice for the victims and the call to embrace the perpetrator. I knew, of course, of easy ways to resolve this powerful tension. But I also knew that they were easy precisely because they were false."[6] Many of us are familiar with such tensions in the Christian life, although we are not always so honest in naming them or admitting that the easy ways to resolve them are counterfeit.

But beyond our personal experience, our most cherished anchors of Christian doctrine themselves exist within paradoxical tensions that the most astute minds of the past two thousand years have struggled to adequately express, let alone resolve:

- God is three and yet one—the paradox of the Trinity.
- Jesus Christ is completely God and yet completely human—the paradox of the incarnation.
- Salvation is a free gift of God's grace and yet somehow does not become personal for me until I respond in faith—the paradox of divine election and human free will.

These tensions must *not* be resolved, for, as any church historian will attest, the major heresies of the past two millennia involve emphasizing one side of these paradoxes to the detriment of the other. Jesus just a little more divine than human, or just a tiny bit more human than divine, is heresy; the true Jesus is the grand paradox, equally and indivisibly God and human. Both practically and doctrinally, Christians must live within such tensions if we are to remain faithful to the biblical revelation, which is far more paradoxical than we sometimes admit.

Solving Problems or Addressing Mystery?

The Western world has been successful at solving problems. Theologian John Leith suggests our "success has been the source of temptation to believe not only that all problems can, in fact as well as in principle, be solved but also that life itself can be understood and handled as a problem."[7] When we think this way, there is no room left for mystery, even God's mystery.

Unlike problems, mystery is unsolvable both in principle and in practice. Problems can be objectified and scrutinized, broken down into manageable pieces for detailed study. Mystery defies objectification. There is no way to get outside mystery to analyze it from an objective vantage point. I can step outside a chemical reaction; I cannot step outside myself in my experience of mystery.

While the appropriate response to problems is study, hard work, and the application of techniques, the appropriate response to mystery is awe and wonder. Once solved, problems can be handled by anyone who learns the correct formula or technique. No formula can be passed from person to person to "solve" a mystery, however. Mystery confronts each of us uniquely and invites exploration rather than mastery. Mystery is inexhaustible. "The more mystery is recognized, the more mysterious and wondrous it becomes."[8]

Life without mystery is sterile. People pound away at computer terminals all day, then gather for Druid worship by the light of the moon. The New Age movement spawned a whole new category of people who are "spiritual but not religious."[9] With half-suppressed smiles, Christians watch their contemporaries seek transcendent reality in the most ludicrous ways. But these efforts are far from comical; they are tragic. British pastor and theologian John Stott asks whether Christian worship today offers "what people are craving—the element of mystery, the 'sense of the numinous,' in biblical language 'the fear of God,' in modern language 'transcendence'?"[10] In today's spiritual marketplace, why do we Christians not already have the market cornered on mystery? Should we not be warning people to "accept no substitutes"?

An Open Door into God's Mystery

We have arrived at the purpose of this book, which is to reclaim and embrace biblical paradox as a means by which we can more fully experience the mystery of God. The essence of paradox is the tension created by bringing seemingly opposite ideas into relationship with each other, and such tensions are prominent throughout Scripture. What I hope to offer are ways we can recognize these paradoxical tensions, reflect on them, and ultimately harness them to open up new horizons in knowing God. Embracing such mystery, I maintain, offers us a strange sort of comfort. In this first section, we will continue to explore the concept of mystery and how it is endemic in Christian life and, particularly, in God.

Part 2, "Serious Playfulness," looks at how Jesus often addressed a serious theme with a playful paradoxical saying, such as, "Whoever wants to save his life must lose it." Jesus is a master at using paradoxical tension to reframe important issues and prod our spiritual imagination. This first-order paradox can ultimately be resolved as we learn to see in new ways.

Part 3, "The Tuning Fork," suggests that some biblical paradoxes exist in harmonic tension, just as the twin tines of a tuning fork vibrate in unison to create one pure note neither can produce by itself. Such second-order paradoxes often express the mystery of our relationship with God.

Part 4, "The Two Handles," begins with my grandfather digging postholes in the hard Nebraska soil only when his hands were on the ends of the opposing handles of his auger. This genre of paradox creates its characteristic tension by keeping two contrasting ideas (like my grandfather's hands) as far apart as possible. This third-order paradox often expresses the mystery of being. Table 1 summarizes these three orders of paradox.

THREE ORDERS OF PARADOX

	Serious Playfulness	Tuning Fork	Two Handles
Key Image	Picture Frame: reframes reality as we look through it	Tuning Fork: both tines must vibrate together to create a new note	Auger: performs best when hands are far apart on opposite handles
Characteristic Tension	Startles us but ultimately dissolves	Keeps polarities in vibration together	Keeps polarities separate and distinct
Representative Examples	• Sayings of Jesus • Kingdom parables[a] • Great reversals[b] • Faith versus works	• Justice/love • Transcendent/personal • Election/free will • God's kingdom	• Humanity • Scripture • Trinity • Jesus Christ
What do we see as we look through it?	Mystery of life in God's kingdom	Mystery of relationships, God's relationship with us and ours with God	Mystery of being, God's being and our being

[a] Parables of the kingdom (e.g., Matt. 13:24–30, 31–32, 33, 44–46, 47–50).
[b] Great reversals (e.g., Mark 9:35; 12:10; Matt. 20:1–16; Mark 9:40; Matt. 12:30; 25:29).

TABLE 1

These three orders (or perhaps genres) of biblical paradox are each distinguished by a characteristic tension. My goal in these sections is not to look *at* biblical paradox (and especially not to try to solve, justify, or rationalize it) but rather to look *through* it to better see what it reveals—a holy, mysterious, awesome God. The strategy is inductive—slowly letting the paradoxes do their work in us. Finally, part 5, "The Shell," offers a deductive counterpoint on why we must engage biblical paradox in our spiritual lives and how to do that.

As we begin, I admit that paradox can be unnerving. While our reason usually first detects paradox, our reason cannot solve it. Some fear that paradox in the Bible equals irrationality. They want clear answers with no waffling or wavering, details spelled out to the last subpoint. Others prefer to approach God's mystery through other avenues: the emotional, the ineffable, the mystic, the charismatic—too much thinking leaves them cold.

Philosopher Ludwig Wittgenstein spent his life analyzing the use and meaning of language. When faced with mystery, he concludes, "My whole tendency . . . was to run against the boundaries of language. This running against the walls of our cage is perfectly, absolutely hopeless. . . . But it is a document of a tendency in the human mind."[11] This is true. As we try to express our paradoxical existence—and especially God's mystery—we do indeed "run against the boundaries of language," and that can easily put us off. Yet Oswald Chambers superbly articulates the other side: "The author who benefits you most is not the one who tells you something you did not know before, but the one who gives expression to the truth that has been dumbly struggling in you for utterance."[12]

Yes, most of us have moments when it would be far easier if someone (pastor, guru, talk radio host) spelled out for us exactly what to believe. Yes, the Christian faith can deteriorate into getting from point A to point B, mindlessly following the robotic instructions of a GPS. And yet . . . there *is* a strange sort of comfort in encountering a mysterious God who is far bigger, grander, and more awesome than we imagined. This is our goal.

Reflection Questions

1. When was the last time you experienced thoughts or feelings similar to those expressed by Cheryl? How did they arise? What, if anything, did you do about them?

2. Have you found peace, as Cheryl finally did, in the fact that "there is a God and I am not he"? If so, how?

3. Does the prospect of exploring biblical paradox sound enticing or scary? Why?

4. "Beyond all question, the mystery from which true godliness springs is great" (1 Tim. 3:16). Does this verse present a red light or a green light to you in exploring the mystery of God? Explain.

Chapter 2

FOG

*The deeper we get into reality, the more numerous will be
the questions we cannot answer.*
—Baron von Hügel, *The Reality of God*

A few weeks after we moved to California's San Joaquin Valley, a family in our new congregation invited us to dinner at their home several miles outside our town. We had been warned about the thick fog that was often a feature of the winter months. As veterans of harsh Chicago and Minneapolis winters, we wondered, "How difficult could a little fog be?" That evening we found out. While we were on our way to the family's home in the countryside, fog closed in around us. No longer could we see landmarks or even street signs. After we spent many minutes following the directions they gave us, a familiar brightly lit intersection loomed out of the fog. We had circled our city and were now approaching from the opposite direction! Chastened, we doggedly started over and found their home on our second try. My recollection of our first night driving in the fog is still vivid: creeping along gravel country roads with my head out the window, straining to see the side of the road and avoid driving my family into the ditch.

Since then I have spent many hours driving in all kinds of fog. Fog can still be unnerving when I drive on unfamiliar roads. When I am in a hurry, I can rue the fog like most people do. Yet fog's mystery has had a growing appeal for me over the years. Now I appreciate fog's eerie ability to hide familiar sights while at the same time revealing them in new ways.

Lampposts, Forests, and Starry Heavens

Mystery is not paradox, but the two are related. If mystery is the goal, paradox is one way to journey into it as I drive into the fog. Theologian E. L. Mascall identifies three features of mystery.[1] First, as with fog, the area in which we have clear vision fades into a vast obscure background. Second, as we attempt to penetrate this background, we slowly understand it is far greater than we realized. Driving in fog, our headlights show us some things clearly but also make us aware of how much exists in the haze. Making a crucial point, Mascall observes, "In the contemplation of a mystery there go together in a remarkable way an increase both of knowledge and also of what we might call conscious ignorance."[2] Third, mystery, while itself remaining obscure, has an uncanny ability to illuminate other things. The same is true of paradox: while it remains obscure and mysterious to us, it illuminates or opens a door into the mystery of God. We will circle back to these three basic components of mystery often in the pages ahead.

In C. S. Lewis's classic *The Lion, the Witch, and the Wardrobe*, Lucy passes through the wardrobe into a world that is similar to, yet very different from, her own. She sees snow on the ground, pine trees, and a lamppost you might find in any London park, yet she soon encounters animals that talk and centaurs and a land where it is always winter but never Christmas. It is the points of familiarity that show how different Narnia truly is. Hence mystery is not simply the unknown. If there were *no* points in common, Narnia for Lucy would not be mysterious and thus exciting to explore; it would instead be bewildering.

A key element in all mystery is that the little we know draws us deeper into, invites a closer inspection of, and engages our imagination about what remains unknown. Roger Hazelton compares it to a forest: "Faith is like a forest which urges us on and deepens, even as it corrects and satisfies, our thought. By its means we never know God and ourselves wholly, yet we know nevertheless truly. We may see in a glass darkly, but we really do see."[3] Standing outside the forest, you observe only a dark wall of trees. However, the farther into the forest you penetrate, discovering clearings and streams and birds, the more acutely you experience its mystery, never knowing wholly, but knowing truly.

Baron von Hügel, perceptive about many matters, including mystery, uses similar imagery: "A sheer conundrum is not mysterious, nor is a blank wall; but forests are mysterious, in which at first you observe but little, yet in which, with time, you see more and more, although never the whole; and the starry heavens are thus mysterious, and the spirit of man, and above all God, our origin and home."[4] A conundrum is not mysterious; it is simply a puzzling dead end. Likewise, a blank wall is not mysterious; nothing is there! But for Von Hügel, the heavens offer an experience similar to that of the forest. Identifying constellations in that immense starry mass engenders greater wonder than a quick glance at the sky. Learning that the light from some stars in those constellations was radiated millions of years ago heightens even more our appreciation of the mystery of the heavens.

In both forests and the heavens, what we discover serves to raise our awareness and appreciation of what we do not know. We are more likely to hike farther and explore the deeper reaches of the forest once we know some paths into it. We are more likely to gaze into the heavens with a telescope once we recognize some constellations. In the same way, the attraction to mystery grows as we penetrate the mystery more deeply. As theologian John Macquarrie suggests, "A mystery is . . . a question in which we only glimpsed the shape or direction of an answer, and found that the more we penetrated into the answer, the more its horizons expanded so that we could never fully grasp it."[5]

Knowing the God We Do Not Know

I love backpacking in the Sierra Nevada Mountains. As I'm climbing a steep ridge, the horizon beckons me onward, until it looks to be only yards in front of me. Just a few more steps will reach it! Yet after those few steps, do I finally meet the horizon? No, those steps to the top of the ridge open up a far greater vista. More ridges and valleys come into view, with the horizon again far in the distance.

We can seem on the verge of having God figured out. Yet when we reach what looked like the summit, a grand new perspective greets us. The climb has increased our knowledge of the terrain (we know God better than we did before), but we now see all the unknown territory reaching outward to the distant new horizon. Theologian John Leith reflects about never reaching that horizon: "Human knowledge may fill the gaps in our knowledge and in our power. Yet the more knowledge and more power we have, the more the horizon recedes. There does not seem to be any escape from the mystery that encompasses us."[6]

When I speak of God's mystery, I have this horizon in mind. Where God is concerned, what we do not know far outweighs what we know. As we have seen, E. L. Mascall provocatively calls this conscious ignorance. Swiss theologian Karl Barth describes it in a no less memorable way: "God remains a mystery even as he reveals himself, for it is as a mystery that he is revealed. Our Christian situation is not that of ignorance or not knowing alone; it is the predicament of knowing what we do not know, and of calling mystery by its right name, God."[7] If "knowing what we do not know" sounds paradoxical, that's because it surely is.

As we penetrate deeper into knowing this mysterious God, we discover that often when we think we have things nailed down and say, "God is this," we must quickly go on to say, "But God is also that." God is transcendent *but also* immanent. God is sovereign *but also* creates humans in his image with genuine freedom. God is perfect love *but also* is perfectly just. God is three *but also* one.

As we drive into the fog, our headlights extend our range of vision and illuminate things previously unseen, but at the same time we recognize that there is a vast, obscure background we cannot yet penetrate. God is mystery. Knowing God means growing in both knowledge and, at the same time, conscious ignorance. Most people are quick to seek knowledge. Few clamor for conscious ignorance. Yet in knowing God, we cannot have one without the other.

As we begin to explore this "known/unknown" paradoxical landscape, Eugene Peterson reminds us that God's mystery is not frightening: "There are necessarily many mysteries that we will never comprehend. (A god you can understand is not God.) But they are good, light-filled mysteries, not ominous evil-tinged mysteries."[8]

Neither is God's mystery irrational. Barth cautions us that we must not wallow in God's mystery but do the best we can to comprehend it: "Theology means taking rational trouble over the mystery. . . . If we are unwilling to take the trouble, neither shall we know what we mean when we say that we are dealing with the mystery of God."[9] Thus, while we can never map the vast wild regions of the mystery of God, if we are willing to take the trouble, we can find rational pathways that lead us into them.

Observers both ancient and modern suggest that one of these pathways is paradox. For all its frustrating aspects that cause us to eye it nervously or throw up our arms and stalk away, paradox has an allure that cannot be denied. Like unusual stones discovered in the bottom of a prospector's pan, some paradoxes keep us coming back to them, as we roll them in our palms, pondering their secrets. Even as postmodern society continues to turn away from organized religion, its fascination with mystery has never been greater. From a hundred different directions, people today avidly seek a spirituality that addresses life's inherent mystery. Christians are well positioned to come alongside them, if only we will recognize that we are sitting on the mother lode of the Mystery that so many are earnestly prospecting for.

An Invitation to Settled Explorers

A party of pioneers entered a new land. Game was plentiful in the verdant forests. Rivers sparkled with enormous trout easily plucked from their glacial waters. The air was pure and sweet. An enormous sky stretched from a green horizon to white-capped peaks. Everywhere the pioneers looked, beauty and majesty beckoned. Everyone agreed it was just the place they had imagined to make a new life for themselves.

After tramping in the dark forests, they sat around their evening campfires and told stories of their explorations. Soon trees were felled and cabins built. Youngest to oldest sweated together, carrying stones out of the meadows so crops could be planted and harvested to sustain them through the long winters.

After the dangers of the trail, creating a settlement was a welcome change. The men still hunted and fished, of course, and the women and children often entered the forest to pick berries or look for mushrooms. But fewer trips into the really wild lands were required; everything needful was now close at hand. Rather than exploring, the settlers went on holiday excursions to familiar places for swimming or picnics. Their early adventurous days in the dark forests and mist-shrouded peaks held wonderful memories, but they had built homesteads and were busy with the tasks of daily life.

In the evenings as they sat in front of their cabins, watching the sun turn the peaks a fiery pink, sometimes they speculated about the wilderness valleys they had never explored. "We should mount a new expedition!" someone would propose, prompting nods all around. Seldom did anything come of it. One summer, the stream running through their valley dried up, throwing the community into disarray and prompting an emergency excursion to its headwaters. Once every year or so, greasy mountain men ambled into the settlement with tantalizing tales of the territory beyond the mountains: forests overpopulated with game, and rivers so thick with fish you could walk across them. While the wilderness still occasionally beckoned to them, most of the people in the community remained content with what they already knew.

———————

If entering into mystery can be imagined as exploring a forest, perhaps this imaginary tale describes how some of us have come to know God. While it is initially exhilarating, few can live under frontier conditions indefinitely. Even Daniel Boone and Davy Crockett built homesteads. But as we settle into a relationship with God after the early excitement of coming to faith, we risk shrinking God down to the size needed to sustain our lives on the homestead. Perhaps we stop exploring the wilder territory of God because we think there is little left to discover.

Or maybe we already have enough of God to satisfy our needs. What will get us to mount a new expedition into the mystery of God?

Paradox gets us exploring because it regularly intrudes into our settled lives; paradox is part of being human and, even more, part of being Christian. Beyond well-worn trails to the creek or woodpile, paradox opens up new paths into the untamed landscape of God that surrounds our settled clearings. "Faith is like a forest which urges us on and deepens, even as it corrects and satisfies, our thought."[10] Every one of us first entered this faith landscape as explorers; settled believers can become explorers again.

Reflection Questions

1. Describe an experience, like driving in the fog, where the mysterious became intriguing rather than frustrating.

2. Has your relationship with God ever involved standing back to observe, question, or wonder? How has this changed you?

3. Have you ever considered that conscious ignorance might be a good thing? How might this be true in relation to God?

4. "Pray for us, too, that God may open a door for our message, so that we may proclaim the mystery of Christ" (Col. 4:3). The New Testament writers often speak of the mystery of God. How has the meaning of this mystery changed for you after reading this chapter?

Chapter 3

NEWTON'S APPLE

*The Scripture's gospel is shallow enough for babes to wade
in and never drown and yet deep enough for scholars to
swim in and never touch bottom.*

—Saint Jerome

In 1687, Sir Isaac Newton developed formulas to explain the behavior of all moving objects. Falling apples and falling stars, the Cambridge University professor discovered, obey the same laws of motion. Principles of universal gravitation apply to spinning tops or spinning planets. The elegant simplicity was breathtaking. Surely, here was the ultimate insight into the God-ordained order of the universe. Unfortunately, a few centuries later Albert Einstein upset Newton's applecart. Apparently, the great seventeenth-century mathematician's equations could not offer exact predictions when velocities increased. Einstein's theory of special relativity proposed that moving objects behave differently when traveling near the speed of light.

Newton was not wrong. His theories are still used for most calculations in the everyday world. Unless you are on the starship *Enterprise* approaching warp speed, Newton's degree of error regarding moving objects is negligible, just as the curvature of the earth is negligible when builders are laying the foundation for a house. Scientists call this acceptable degree of accuracy a "domain of validity."[1] Within their domain of validity, Newton's theories of motion are actually better than Einstein's, because they are far simpler to use for everyday needs (even though in high school many of us did not care which of the two trains moving at different speeds reached the station first).

Think of our everyday distinction between matter and energy. Because of the low energy states of most matter around us, we assume matter is matter and energy is energy. Chemistry classes still teach the law of conservation of mass: in burning wood, for example, the total mass after the process is completed must equal the total mass before the process began. Matter can in fact be converted into energy, as predicted by Einstein's most famous equation, $E = mc^2$, yet seldom do we think of matter as another form of energy. In our daily lives (and in the chemistry lab), the law of conservation of mass has an appropriate domain of validity.

In the twentieth century, a scientific revolution even greater than Newton's profoundly changed how we understand our world. It was quantum mechanics. Subatomic particles do not follow the laws of classical Newtonian physics but behave in quite aberrant and even whimsical ways. Fritz Rohrlich speaks to the challenges of moving from the familiar world of classical Newtonian physics to quantum mechanics: "There is no reason other than prejudice to expect the quantum world to be expressible in classical terms. Since that world is admittedly strange to us, being very far removed from our experience, it should come as no surprise that many of the problems we have in comprehending it are due to our lack of proper words for its new and unfamiliar concepts and for its peculiar nature. *The analogies we can draw to the world we are familiar with are in general rather poor.* . . . This is why the quantum world offers a very special challenge" (emphasis added).[2]

What first led to discovering this quantum world is the familiar paradox of light, which can be partly explained by the properties of a wave but has other behavior consistent with particles. This "wave/particle" paradox makes no sense as long as we evaluate it with Newtonian concepts that define what we mean by "sense." Hence, to comprehend this new subatomic world, we make a paradigm shift[3] away from analogies from the world we know (classical Newtonian physics) to be guided by different (quantum) concepts appropriate to this new and very different world.

Levels of Reality

Newtonian and quantum physics introduce us to levels of reality. Because nature is complex, to study something carefully, we must ignore some aspects in order to concentrate on others. Take Newton's apple. A botanist might study the texture of the fruit, a molecular biologist the cell composition, a physicist the atomic structure, and a theoretical physicist the behavior of particles that make up its atoms. All these scientists have the same reality in view, but each is concerned with a different level. Scientists call this *idealizing*: shrinking a complex system into a simpler (ideal) system to study selected aspects. The botanist never thinks about the atoms that compose the apple, while the theoretical physicist couldn't care less whether the atoms being studied came from an apple or a Chippendale chair.[4] A traffic engineer studies the movement of cars during rush-hour traffic but couldn't care less how well each car engine functions; an auto mechanic is focused on tuning a car's engine but couldn't care less where it is driven during rush hour.

As we seek to know God, could there be different levels of reality, just as there are in the physical world? I think this is quite possible. Such a notion should not be used to promote false spiritual hierarchies, whether the age-old strains of Gnosticism offering secret knowledge to the specially initiated or the more modern hierarchies based on spiritual gifts. The levels I want to think about are available to anyone with the simple desire to explore them; as with the scientists with Newton's apple or the traffic engineer and the auto mechanic, it all depends on where we focus.

On one level, God has certainly revealed all we need to know for human salvation—the life, death, and resurrection of Jesus Christ. As with the classical world of Newtonian physics, most Christians operate within this framework most of the time. When asked for his definition of the gospel, Karl Barth, theological giant of the twentieth century, is said to have replied, "Jesus loves me, this I know, for the Bible tells me so!"

But as with Newtonian physics, it is dangerous to assume this is *all* there is. Einstein and others showed that reality has deeper mysteries. The quantum world did not mesh well with what classical physics had come to expect, and while this new world was not irrational, it was rational in a way never before considered (or different from what Newton might have defined as rational). If God created reality in such a way that the subatomic world operates on a completely different set of principles than the world we see and touch, why might the same not be true in the realm of the Spirit? And if the paradoxes discovered in natural phenomena (light exhibiting properties of both particles and waves, for example) stimulated the exploring instincts of scientific seekers, why might biblical paradox not do the same for spiritual seekers?[5] Saint Jerome might have had a notion of such levels of reality in mind: "The Scripture's gospel is shallow enough for babes to wade in and never drown and yet deep enough for scholars to swim in and never touch bottom."

Think of the Newtonian spiritual truth "Jesus died for our sins." Shallow enough for babes. But when I made the point with my students that the triune God—Father, Son, and Spirit—are *all* involved in redemption, suddenly things got complicated. "If God was in heaven, how could God also be dying on the cross?" With our worldview shaped by a space/time universe, it seems impossible that God could be in two places at once. In fact, the statement "Jesus died for our sins" might honestly be called an *idealization*—a focus on the big picture of salvation while not considering other levels of reality. The paradox of the Trinity opens up all sorts of issues for scholars to swim in and never touch bottom. Indeed, they have been doing so for centuries!

A Quantum World of the Spirit

James Gleick, in his bestselling *Chaos: Making a New Science*, shows how chaos theory has forced us to change our views of reality: "Nonlinear systems with real chaos were rarely taught and rarely learned. When people stumbled across such things—and people did—all their training argued for dismissing them as aberrations. Only a few were able to remember that the solvable, orderly, linear systems were the aberrations. Only a few, that is, understood how nonlinear nature is in its soul."[6] If the soul of creation is indeed nonlinear (not straightforward or orderly), what might this say about its Creator?

Does not our experience with God push us toward a quantum world of the Spirit? We are frustrated that God's help does not arrive as we hope it will, then are surprised when it shows up in totally unexpected ways. We find comfortable answers about how God works in our lives, only to discover new questions we cannot ignore lurking beneath our answers. Might we find we have accumulated solid evidence for the ways God functions as waves, only to bump into equally compelling evidence for the ways God functions as particles?

This prompts me to ask, Do the familiar Christian beliefs we employ in daily living also have a domain of validity? Remember, a domain of validity shows us when our questions fall outside its boundaries. Might the mystery of God exist as a level of reality alongside (or within or underneath) our familiar beliefs? Indeed, a quantum world of the Spirit might be waiting to be discovered, with paradox first catching our attention (as the contradictory properties of light alerted physicists) regarding this new level of reality. Some apples might fall farther from the tree than Newton expected.

Reflection Questions

1. This chapter uses an analogy from discoveries about physical reality to suggest that different levels of reality might also exist in the spiritual realm. Do you find this possibility threatening or stimulating? How so?

2. We know that paradox in natural phenomena (for example, the strange properties of light) forced scientists to go deeper, exploring different levels of reality. As you have encountered paradox in your spiritual journey, how has it forced you to go deeper?

3. Can you think of any examples of different domains of validity in the Christian life, whereby the answers that work on one level are not adequate for a deeper level? Might spiritual growth be imagined as moving from one level to explore another one?

4. Is it fair or honest to apply analogies from the physical world to the spiritual world? Why or why not?

PART 2

SERIOUS PLAYFULNESS

Chapter 4

SERIOUS PLAYFULNESS

*What Christ said was true, but it was never a truism. The
escape from truism came by the consistent employment of
paradox in which there is always a hint of the laughable.*
—Elton Trueblood, *The Humor of Christ*

Would Jesus of Nazareth emerge in our era as a megachurch preacher?
One wonders. Would he dismiss megachurches, as some people do,
simply because they attract large numbers? Certainly, Jesus preached
to big crowds. Add to this that Jesus spoke with authority; he had the
charisma often associated with megawatt preachers. He could pack
them in. At least in the beginning.

Imagine this scenario. A well-known preacher has just finished a
sermon heard by thousands in a huge amphitheater and by thousands
more via cable TV. The one-hundred-voice choir, backed by a twenty-
piece orchestra and cutting-edge technology, has sent people away with
a stirring musical climax. The preacher is walking out a backstage door
when a dozen key backers, who have been with him since he was a
complete unknown, corner him. "Tell us again," they ask. "What *exactly*
were you trying to say this morning? We didn't understand a thing!"
I suspect such an admission (or accusation) would be devastating to
the preacher's credibility. Yet this is exactly how Jesus' own disciples
approached him on several occasions (for example, Matt. 13:36–43).
How long would any megachurch preacher last if people went away
scratching their heads?

So axiomatic is today's omnipresent emphasis on clarity—"If the trumpet does not sound a clear call, who will get ready for battle?" (1 Cor. 14:8)—that it startles us to discover that Jesus was not overly concerned if people did not always get it. At times, Jesus was clear and pointed—indeed uncomfortably so, for his original audience and for us. But we miss a major element of Jesus' preaching if we fail to recognize that he was quite willing to be paradoxical. He left listeners puzzled and perturbed, with dangling loose ends and no easy resolutions. Often his words or parables proposed contradictions. Seldom, if ever, did Jesus' preaching have a fill-in-the-blank directness that in some circles today is an assumed sign of good communication.

Playful Paradox

New Testament scholar Robert Stein identifies many literary forms Jesus uses to startle and entice his listeners, including paradox.[1] Usually Jesus' words are paradoxical in the ancient Greek sense of violating usual categories or going against the grain. This is quite different from the paradox to be discussed in parts 3 and 4, where truth resides within the tension created between opposing assertions. If we use our earlier definition of paradox as "anything which is intellectually objection-able but nevertheless unavoidable,"[2] Jesus' paradoxes may indeed be intellectually objectionable, but they are *not*, ultimately, unavoidable or irresolvable. I call them *playful* paradoxes because they play with traditional ideas, worldviews, or attitudes, often juxtaposing contrasting ideas to get us to respond in new ways. Even more, they playfully confront our often overly serious approach to living the life Jesus has for us.

As I began exploring Jesus' use of paradox, I was also surveying what academia has to say about paradox. I discovered a rich vein of insight into Jesus' methods in an unexpected place: modern psychology. Viktor Frankl, the renowned Viennese creator of logotherapy, which was birthed during his experience in a World War II concentration camp, wrote about "paradoxical intention" in his treatment of compulsions and phobias.[3] Since that beginning, "therapeutic paradox" has proliferated and become something of a buzzword.[4] Unlike traditional psychotherapy, paradoxical strategies do not assume that change results from insight into hidden impulses, memories, or feelings. Rather, change is a result of doing things differently.[5] Clients are cajoled into new ways of acting, the premise being that how we *act* eventually influences how we *are*. For example, a client who sweats profusely before leading a business meeting is instructed to try to produce even more perspiration; an agoraphobic is told to spend even more time in shopping malls; a compulsive hand washer is advised to wash her hands an extra twenty times a day.

The primary therapeutic paradox strategies are paradoxical intention and reframing. These are two conceptual maps by which we can better understand how Jesus' playful use of paradox leads to change, and why it does not lead to change if we squeeze out all the paradox and take it too seriously. We will look through the lens of each strategy in the next two chapters.

Playful Paradox and Systems Change

As a beginning, however, it is important to note the distinction that systems theorists make between first- and second-order change.[6] Human beings are part of many overlapping systems, including country, region, community, church, family, person, and finally each person's own worldview. First-order change happens within a system; second-order change, by contrast, originates from outside a system with the hope of changing the system.

Nightmares offer a simple example. To escape the fearful presence, a person might hide, fight back, or run—these are first-order changes because they happen within the dream. A second-order change—changing the system itself—is waking up! Systems theory suggests that many issues we face require second-order change—change that originates from outside the system. For example, an individual within a family can begin acting differently when the family system in which she is living begins to change. A family enmeshed in anger and destructive behavior begins to change when the child's teacher invites Mom and Dad to attend free parenting classes at the school. A church that peremptorily fired its last three pastors has a more successful pastorate after inviting an outside consultant to hold up a mirror in which it can see its dysfunctional issues.

Our natural responses to most challenges are first-order solutions; we confine our thinking to the system in which the challenges originate. A family seeks to solve its conflicts without consulting an outside counselor; a city seeks to solve its drug problem without thinking about where the drugs come from; a state seeks to improve air quality without addressing sources of pollution throughout the region; a nation seeks to expand its economy without considering the trade policies of neighboring countries. If a person struggles with insomnia, first-order solutions might be practicing relaxation techniques or drinking a glass of warm milk before bed. However, some first-order solutions can exacerbate or even *become* the problem—for example, the person trying to will himself to sleep, which only increases the anxiety that makes sleep impossible. Paradoxically, a second-order solution to insomnia might be someone telling the person to try to remain awake all night; the anxiety of not being able to sleep slowly dissipates, allowing sleep to come.[7] For lasting change, we often need intervention from outside the system where the challenges occur: "Second-order solutions are often viewed from within the system as unpredictable, amazing, and surprising, since they are not necessarily based on the rules and assumptions of that system."[8]

We can begin to appreciate any number of Jesus' paradoxical sayings as promoting second-order change. They come across as "unpredictable, amazing, or surprising" precisely because they originate outside his audience's worldview. Elton Trueblood puts it well: "Christ seems to employ exactly that amount of shock which is necessary to make people break through their deeply ingrained obtuseness."[9] Paradox explodes assumptions that imprison us within a system.

In first-century Palestine, greatness was measured by *having* servants, not *being* a servant. "Not so with you. Instead, whoever wants to become great among you must be your servant, and whoever wants to be first must be slave of all" (Mark 10:43–44). "Sitting down, Jesus called the Twelve and said, 'Anyone who wants to be first must be the very last, and the servant of all'" (Mark 9:35). Viewed from within Jesus' first-century cultural system, the idea that the very last will end up first is downright delusional. Jesus steps outside the assumptions of this system to state a new definition of greatness in his kingdom.

"Truly I tell you, among those born of women there has not risen anyone greater than John the Baptist; yet whoever is least in the kingdom of heaven is greater than he" (Matt. 11:11). John the Baptist is greatest within the first-order system of "those born of women." Yet the kingdom of God is a more comprehensive system, now arriving as a whole new order of reality. What a surprise to John's disciples!

"Take the bag of gold from him and give it to the one who has ten bags. For whoever has will be given more, and they will have an abundance. Whoever does not have, even what they have will be taken from them" (Matt. 25:28–29). This paradoxical conclusion to the parable of the bags of gold (Matt. 25:14–30) is a classic reversal of expectations. God's kingdom, so seemingly unfair in our eyes, explodes the rules and assumptions of our system.

"Truly I tell you, unless you change and become like little children, you will never enter the kingdom of heaven. Therefore, whoever takes the lowly position of this child is the greatest in the kingdom of heaven" (Matt. 18:3–4). The first-century Jewish view of children was the polar opposite of our modern, sometimes-romanticized view. Robert Stein explains, "Children were not thought of in Judaism as innocent unspoiled children of God. On the contrary, they were thought of as under the fall of Adam, possessing an evil inclination and without help until they became a bar mitzvah at the age of thirteen and received the help of the law."[10] How shocking that to become such an evil child was the pathway to greatness!

"Do not suppose that I have come to bring peace to the earth. I did not come to bring peace, but a sword. For I have come to turn 'a man against his father, a daughter against her mother, a daughter-in-law against her mother-in-law'" (Matt. 10:34–35). The expected Messiah was to lead "us" (Israel) against "them" (Romans), not create such painful divisions within "us"! Once again, Jesus exposes in a dramatic way the high stakes in following him.

In these examples (and in Jesus' use of paradox in general), the contrasting assertions forming the paradox are within the same saying (for example, "Whoever wants to be *first* must be *slave*" [Mark 10:44, emphasis added]; "Whoever *takes the lowly position* of this child is the *greatest*" [Matt. 18:4, emphasis added]).[11] Ultimately, the paradox is resolved as it succeeds in opening our minds to second-order change. As we will discover in the next chapters, Jesus' playful use of paradox has a serious purpose.

Reflection Questions

1. Have you ever thought of Jesus as playful? Can you incorporate such an idea into your mental picture of him? What might need to change in order for you to do so?

2. Think of an experience or problem where you kept trying first-order solutions that were not successful, then discovered a second-order change that came from outside the system.

3. After reading this chapter, how might you approach one of Jesus' paradoxical sayings differently?

4. How might the playfulness of Jesus be contrasted with the seriousness of the Pharisees? Don't they criticize Jesus because he does not seem to take his religion as seriously as they do? What new insights does this stimulate in you?

Chapter 5

TRY HARDER!

> *If we assume that any chronic condition that we are*
> *persistently trying to change will, perversely, be supported*
> not to change *by our serious efforts to bring about change,*
> *then it is logical to consider the possibility that one way out*
> *of this paradox is to be paradoxical.*
> —Edwin H. Friedman, *Generation to Generation*

I was sitting in my supervisor's cramped office, once again regretting my decision to forgo my seminary classes in favor of a semester working as an intern chaplain at a large metropolitan medical center. Called Clinical Pastoral Education (CPE), the program entailed forty hours a week of hands-on experience visiting patients, buttressed by weekly feedback sessions with my supervisor. I thought this plunge into the deep end of the pool would help me learn to swim as a pastor; often, however, I had no idea what to say to patients or, even worse, how to say it. Far more comfortable in libraries, I was clearly out of my depth dealing with the emotions that overflowed every hospital room. An even more anxious part of the experience, however, was the weekly encounter-style supervision meetings that I approached with dry-mouthed vulnerability.

Unexpectedly, my supervisor said, "Rich, I think you should try harder." I was shocked. No one had ever accused me of not trying hard enough, in anything. I am conscientious to the core. I suffered his reproach in silence. Yet at our next weekly meeting, he said it again.

"Rich, why aren't you trying harder?" Now my anxiety really spiked! Even the one person in the hospital with whom I felt relatively safe thought I was failing! I replied in total sincerity, "But I *am* trying hard!" His only reply: "I think you should try harder." After this same advice was given for a third week in a row, I finally boiled over: "I've been trying as hard as I can all semester, and I can't try any harder! You know what? I give up!" He smiled kindly, his eyes twinkling, and said only one word. "Good."

Chinese Handcuffs

Whether we are dealing with change in ourselves or seeking to promote change in others, trying harder is like struggling to escape from Chinese handcuffs: the harder you attempt to pull your fingers apart, the tighter the handcuffs become. Only by playing with the handcuffs do you discover that pushing both fingers together (the opposite of trying harder) releases them. My supervisor had correctly diagnosed that my try-harder anxiety to prove myself was impeding my relationships with both my patients and my colleagues. He employed Viktor Frankl's technique of "paradoxical intention": "The therapist encourages the client to maintain, with great vigor, the problem behavior at its presenting level or, if possible, at a level that is even more discomforting."[1] This method is also called symptom prescription. Clients are "prescribed" their own anxiety-provoking symptoms in exaggerated ways. An agoraphobic, for example, might be advised to methodically increase time spent in crowds. A compulsive hand washer might be told to wash his hands an extra twenty times a day. This seemingly silly paradoxical advice has a serious purpose. "The client's emotional response to paradox (e.g., shock, surprise, confusion) may serve as a positive therapeutic experience."[2]

As we discussed in the last chapter, our first response to challenges is often to double down and try harder within the existing system. Saul is a poster child for this: "circumcised on the eighth day, of the people of Israel, of the tribe of Benjamin, a Hebrew born of Hebrews;

as to the law a Pharisee" (Phil. 3:5 RSV). No wonder people who lived in simple faith in Jesus incensed Saul. How blasphemous to assume that such a weighty goal as righteousness before God could be secured with so little effort, especially compared with how hard *he* tried! Just as first-order solutions can exacerbate the problem, so Saul's pursuit of righteousness through keeping the law was counterproductive (Gal. 2–3; Rom. 3–4). His encounter with Jesus on the Damascus Road is a classic second-order change. Talk about an outside intervention that brings shock, surprise, and confusion! Saul breaks out of his pharisaical quest for righteousness to become Paul, the apostle of justification by grace through faith.[3]

While Paul is a classic example, Scripture provides others. Consider King Solomon's symptom prescription of offering to settle the rival mothers' dispute by cutting the baby in half (1 Kings 3:16–28). Such a paradoxical approach generated shock, surprise, and confusion that quickly changed the system: each professing mother reveals how much she actually loves the child. It could be argued that the father in one of Jesus' most famous parables practices symptom prescription by giving his prodigal son his inheritance in cash so he might experience the bitter dregs of his rebellious nature and come to his senses in a way he might never have done had he remained chafing in his father's house (Luke 15:11–32).

Detouring around the Maginot Line

My try-harder nature was only temporarily assuaged during my hospital chaplaincy. A decade later I suffered recurring bouts of depression because the church I served was not growing numerically as I had hoped. Again, trying harder was not working. I felt impotent, especially when I watched speakers strut the latest fashion of "proven success" down the runways of church-growth conferences. I returned from every conference so depressed that my wife forbade me from attending them. As I was drowning in my unfulfilled expectations, God threw me a lifeline in the person of systems therapist Edwin Friedman.

First, I learned about seriousness and the liabilities of trying harder.[4] Friedman writes in *Generation to Generation: Family Process in Church and Synagogue*, "If we assume that any chronic condition that we are persistently trying to change will, perversely, be supported *not to change* by our serious efforts to bring about change, then it is logical to consider the possibility that one way out of this paradox is to be paradoxical."[5]

Slowly I came to accept that my serious effort undermined everything; the harder I tried to change people, the less they changed. The alternative is playfulness, Friedman suggests. "If it is generally true that it is not possible to be playful with those for whom we feel too responsible, it is especially true when we feel a responsibility for their salvation! Few religious traditions make much of playfulness."[6]

We can safely assume Jesus is serious about making disciples for the kingdom of God. How then can he engage in so much paradoxical playfulness? Why does he not try harder to tell it like it is? Jesus often leaves his listeners, and us, grappling with dissonance, struggling with the paradoxical tensions he creates; he makes us connect the dots on our own. As we will soon see, Jesus' parables and stories often challenge fixed assumptions and hardened worldviews without head-on confrontation; they are open-ended, forcing us to construct our own endings.

For most of my "serious" life, I never questioned my assumption that change happened through marshalling evidence and logic. Then Friedman taught me the difference between content and process. Often the emotional or relational process is far more influential than persuasive content.[7] How else, for example, do we explain the unusually high percentage of Americans who refuse to accept the reality of manmade climate change even though 97 percent of the world's climate scientists present overwhelming evidence for it?[8]

Most of us have a built-in Maginot Line, similar to the impenetrable system of barriers and bunkers France built to protect itself from Germany after World War I. When someone challenges our worldview, klaxons sound and bunker walls are manned. The invasion of France in World War II began not with a futile frontal attack against the Maginot Line but with German panzer divisions racing in a sweeping detour around the line through undefended Belgium. France fell swiftly. To connect with others, sometimes we need to find a detour around their Maginot Line.

Analyzing communication dynamics, Friedman comments, "It is less the words than the emotional envelope in which they are delivered."[9] My serious, try-harder envelope was often left on the hall table, unopened. Jesus, by contrast, is a classic "non-anxious presence," presenting his message but allowing listeners the emotional freedom to respond or not.[10] In other words, Jesus does not take responsibility for people but makes them responsible for their own spiritual welfare. After he tells the rich young ruler to "sell everything you have and give to the poor" (Mark 10:21), Jesus watches him walk sadly away. (I would have chased after him, saying, "Wait! Let me explain that again!") When a man promises to follow Jesus but asks him to "first let me go and bury my father" (Matt. 8:21), Jesus says it's now or never. (I would have said, "Great! When might I expect you?")

Playful Humor

In his groundbreaking work on therapeutic paradox, Viktor Frankl suggests that the value of paradoxical intention can be heightened through exaggerated or ludicrous humor. A man fearful that his colleagues might assume he could not handle pressure because he sweated profusely during meetings was told to "show his audience what perspiration is really like, to perspire in gushes of drenching torrents of sweat."[11]

We often miss Jesus' use of humor; humor seems so out of place in the supremely serious role of Savior of the world. I'll never forget watching a video of Matthew's gospel[12] and for the first time in my life encountering a Jesus who delivered many of his lines while smiling, laughing (a lot!), and—an even bigger surprise—making other people laugh as well. Consider his observation, "It is easier for a camel to go through the eye of a needle than for someone who is rich to enter the kingdom of God" (Matt. 19:24). This is paradoxical intention at its best, creating shock, surprise, and confusion (perhaps along with some grins) so that the disciples cry out, "Who then can be saved?" (v. 25).

In his masterful little book *The Humor of Christ*, Elton Trueblood concludes, "Of all the mistakes which we make in regard to the humor of Christ, perhaps the worst mistake is our failure, or our unwillingness, to recognize that Christ used deliberately preposterous statements to get his point across."[13] We are not used to thinking of Jesus as playfully preposterous. "The playful," Trueblood continues, "when interpreted with humorless seriousness, becomes merely ridiculous."[14] Trueblood catalogs a host of examples of Jesus' humor, such as the overscrupulous Pharisees who "strain out a gnat but swallow a camel" (Matt. 23:24). I never thought of Jesus as a teaser until I noticed him ask the crowd about the locust-eating, animal-skin-clad John the Baptist, "What did you go out to see? A man dressed in fine clothes?" (Luke 7:25). Trueblood's comment on this teasing Jesus underlines the intent of all his humor: "The teasing and ironical question was certain to be more effective than would have been a wholly serious and indicative approach."[15]

I began asking myself about *my* audience. What do people expect me to say before I even say it? (They know the issues I am most serious about.) How can I shock or surprise them? What is the last thing they expect me to say? How can I be playful?

In a sermon on God's destruction of Sodom, I began my playful detour around my congregation's Maginot Line by describing in great detail how people were so looking forward to the Lord's impending judgment, they built grandstands on the hills above that evil city. With football stadium fervor, they waved banners, stamped their feet, and chanted, "Go, God! Crush Sodom!" Abraham, however, was not in front of the stands cheerleading but standing apart from the raucous crowds, praying for Sodom. Why? Sodom included Lot, his nephew. For Abraham, Sodom could never be a monolithic "them," those evil people. There is a little of "us" in Sodom. Realizing this prompts us to ask for God's mercy, just like Abraham did, rather than cheer for God's judgment. (One conservative central California farmer who did *not* take the detour said to me as I was shaking hands afterward, "While you were preaching, all I could think about was wishing God would push the whole city of San Francisco into the ocean!")

I have learned from Jesus that playfulness is an emotional envelope in which to deliver difficult truths. Intentional playfulness frees me from trying too hard to make an impact or get others to change. It siphons off my responsibility that people "get" the message. This changes the whole emotional triangle involving the people, the message, and me. I become a non-anxious presence. People are free to listen without activating their defenses. And paradoxically, when I am less serious, even intentionally paradoxical, the possibility for impact increases. All this we see in the serious playfulness of Jesus.

Reflection Questions

1. The author's effort to try harder, especially in areas where he was anxious to succeed, became a self-defeating downward spiral. Have you ever experienced this consequence of being overly serious?

2. How do you feel about passages where Jesus seems to speak so obscurely that people are left confused, or where he lets people walk away from him too easily?

3. Is it hard to imagine Jesus laughing, telling a joke, or playfully bantering with people? How could humor be an important dimension of Jesus' character?

4. Reflect on the idea that it is difficult to be playful with people for whom we feel the most responsible, or with the ones we are the most serious about changing. Does this remind you of any relationships in your life—children, spouse, friends, colleagues? How are people resisting your efforts to guide, mentor, or influence them?

Chapter 6

NEW FRAMES

Jesus spoke in parables not only to disclose truth but also to disclose the heart of the listener, to see how much that listener wanted to pursue the truth.

—Ravi Zacharias, "Reaching the Happy Thinking Pagan"

I was wandering around the Rijksmuseum in Amsterdam, on the hunt for the Dutch masters for whom this museum is justly famous. As I entered one of the galleries, I was drawn to a large painting in an intricately carved, gilded frame. The artist was unknown to me. Disappointedly looking to my left at what seemed to be some smaller, nondescript paintings, I realized as I read the card beside each work that I had stumbled into a wealth of Rembrandts. Their simple, unobtrusive frames let Rembrandt's renowned mastery of light penetrating darkness shine to maximum effect.

Frames determine not only what catches our attention, but also how we see it. Tom Sawyer recruits friends who gladly volunteer to paint a fence (work he was supposed to do) because he frames the job so attractively. He begins by pretending he likes the work. "Like it?" he tells his first victim. "Well, I don't see why I oughtn't to like it. Does a boy get a chance to whitewash a fence every day?"[1] Tom continues his guise by daintily brushing the fence and stepping back like an artist appreciating his masterpiece. His friend gets more and more absorbed, until he blurts out, "Say, Tom, let me whitewash a little."[2] Not only is the fence whitewashed; Tom whitewashes the hard work of painting into something his buddies find irresistible.[3]

A new frame changes perception. In ordinary conversation, we ask others to "look at it this way." Media spin doctors have always reframed political events in ways most flattering to their clients. "How should we frame it?" is now the question people in all walks of life ask about all manner of things.

Identified Patients

A bride came to see her pastor several weeks before her wedding, concerned because she was having dreams about men other than her fiancé. Presenting herself as tired, nervous, and depressed, she worried that something was deeply wrong with her. Rather than focus on her depression, however, the minister asked about her relationships. Her fiancé's former wife, whom she had never met, was hostile. Her fiancé seemed incapable of standing up to his former wife, especially on issues regarding their daughter. The minister counseled the bride to think of the depression not as *her* problem but as a function of her fiancé's relationship with his former wife. To extricate herself from this emotional triangle, she was coached to write his former wife a gracious note asking for advice on caring for her soon-to-be stepdaughter. At the rehearsal dinner two weeks later, the bride looked radiant. Depression had evaporated. Much to everyone's delight and surprise, the former wife caused no fuss about allowing her daughter to attend the wedding.[4]

In family systems thinking, the person exhibiting a symptom, such as the bride's depression, is called the "identified patient." Paradoxically, the identified patient is usually not the one with the problem, or at least not *all* the problem. A client is encouraged to perceive a problematic situation through a new frame, to conceive it in a new way.[5] In this example, when the bride exited the emotional triangle between herself, her fiancé, and his former wife, her symptoms "miraculously" disappeared. Her new husband was soon counseling with the same pastor, however; once his bride was no longer the outlet for his tension with his former wife, he felt the full force of this conflict and needed help himself!

An incorrigible child or alcoholic father labeled as the identified patient by the rest of the family might be the only glue holding the family together. Paradoxically, the person creating the most trouble may be *more* invested in the family than the other supposedly well-functioning members. When other family members see the identified patient through this new frame, hopefully they spend less energy fixing (or enabling) the troublemaker and more energy taking responsibility for their own behavior. Even more paradoxically, as they ignore the one with the problem who needs their help and focus on themselves, the identified patient's behavior often improves dramatically. The family system grows healthier when everyone in the family sees his or her interactions with everyone else through a new frame.

Reframing and Jesus

First-century Jews believed wealth was a sure sign of God's favor. Yet Jesus paradoxically reframes the wealth of the rich young ruler as a hindrance he must discard to gain the kingdom of God (Matt. 19:16–30). In the Sermon on the Mount, the Beatitudes paradoxically reframe commonly assumed blessings and curses; it is a blessing to mourn, to be meek, to be reviled, but a curse (especially in Luke's version) to be rich, well fed, or popular (Matt. 5:3–10; Luke 6:20–26). Jesus again and again reframes Jewish law by moving his focus beyond overt acts to inner intentions and attitudes: "Anyone who looks at a woman lustfully has already committed adultery with her in his heart" (Matt. 5:28). Jesus' call to discipleship startles us by reframing traditional notions of commitment: "If anyone comes to me and does not hate father and mother, wife and children, brothers and sisters—yes, even their own life—such a person cannot be my disciple" (Luke 14:26).

On the Damascus Road, Jesus reframes reality for Saul. "'Saul, Saul, why do you persecute me?' 'Who are you, Lord?' Saul asked. 'I am Jesus, whom you are persecuting,' he replied" (Acts 9:4–5). Reality is reframed: the God Saul intended to honor by persecuting Christians is the one Saul is actually persecuting. In psychological jargon, Saul changes class membership: "What makes reframing such an effective tool of change is that once we do perceive the alternative class membership, we cannot so easily go back to the trap and anguish of a former view of reality."[6] Saul had been secure in a Jewish worldview, a class membership he must now reject because membership in a whole new reality centered in Jesus is opening up before him. His letter to the Galatians especially makes this clear (Gal. 2:16–3:14; see also Rom. 3:19–8:39). In a similar way, Jesus reframes reality for error-prone Simon by giving him a new conception of himself as the Rock (Peter).

Reframing has maximum impact when we hold up a new frame and invite an observer to look *through* it. Imagine these comments from an art museum tour guide: "Look at this exquisite frame made of gilded wood in seventeenth-century French baroque style. Notice the intricately carved, leaf-shaped highlights in the corners which finely balance the strong scrollwork along the horizontal axis." She has said a lot about the frame but ignored its *purpose*, which is to focus attention on the painting it surrounds. When a frame does its work well, it is invisible.

Jesus' paradoxical sayings reframe following God by not drawing attention to themselves. When Jesus says, "Whoever wants to save their life will lose it, but whoever loses their life for me will find it" (Matt. 16:25), our attention is quickly drawn away from the paradoxical saying per se, because it reframes all we have ever thought about hedging our bets, playing it safe, not taking risks. Looking through this new window—where "losing" paradoxically becomes "saving"—generates new thoughts in us. What "save my life" behaviors might be hindering my response to Jesus? What do I need to lose to become Jesus' disciple? Rather than offering answers, this new frame prods us to search for answers.

Reframing happens best when we move from being passive observers to active participants. Our typical assumption about change, bequeathed to us by Greek philosophy, follows a theory/behavior or insight/action model: better theory leads to better behavior; better insight leads to better action.[7] Thus our sermons end with applications; we must tell people how to put the sermon's insights into practice. This is classic deductive style: stating general principles, then giving a specific application. But, as many have pointed out,[8] Jesus' preaching is often far more *inductive*, rarely presenting a point-by-point outline but rather wooing listeners into an experience.

This Is *My* Story!

Paradox is therapeutic because it pushes us into action. We saw how paradoxical intention works by increasing a negative behavior ("Try harder!") until it can no longer be sustained. Reframing functions in a similar manner. When others in the system begin acting differently, the identified patient gets better. In both paradoxical intention and reframing, theory or insight is bypassed. In both cases, there is never a completely rational explanation for the positive results. Both cases promote second-order change—the intervention of an outside stimulus breaks open a previously closed system.

Stories can offer this stimulus. When we listen to a story, we are in fact *doing something*, just as therapeutic paradox requires. We try on the roles the story creates for us. The more engaging the story, the more we stop analyzing and simply enter into it, seeing life through the new frame the story creates. Much commentary on Jesus' parables insists that we must be drawn into the story and be caught in the surprise of recognition; only then does the story have its intended impact. Eugene Peterson says it well: "A parable is not an explanation. A parable is not an illustration. We cannot look at a parable as a spectator and expect to get it. A parable does not make a thing easier; it makes it harder by requiring participation, by entering the story."[9] Especially when stories are left open-ended, as many of Jesus' are, we must discover our own ending, because suddenly it is *our* story. This delivers the jolt that reframes our thinking.

I suspect none of the Pharisees listening to Jesus saw themselves as the identified patient, the prodigal son (Luke 15:11–16). Since it was not *their* story, they could listen as spectators, disdaining the prodigal's rebellion and happy he suffered the consequences. In fact, the prodigal sounded a lot like the moral and spiritual riffraff whom Jesus unexpectedly welcomed into his fellowship. But Jesus catches the Pharisees off guard by introducing the elder brother, who represents them and is the real focus of the story. Will the Pharisees now look through the story and see themselves—elder brothers always present with the father yet never really comprehending the father's compassion or mercy (Luke 15:25–32)? Jesus leaves the story open-ended. Will the elder brother come to *his* senses (as his younger brother did) and join his father and prodigal brother at the welcome-home party? As the context makes clear (Luke 15:1–2), Jesus tells this story at the very moment he is throwing a welcome-home party for tax collectors and sinners (younger brothers). Will the Pharisees join the party and Jesus' fellowship or remain outside sulking?

Like the Pharisees, we struggle to allow Jesus' stories to reframe our world. When we observe the self-congratulating Pharisee and breast-beating tax collector praying side by side in the temple (Luke 18:9–14), few of us see ourselves in the preening Pharisee. Neither do we assume we are the oblivious rich man building bigger barns (Luke 12:13–21), cheer for the despicable steward who has an enormous debt forgiven only to throw his fellow servant into prison for a pittance (Matt. 18:21–35), or identify with the obnoxious wedding guest pushing her way forward to the best seat at the marriage feast (Luke 14:7–14). We know an identified patient when we see one! Most of the time, we listen as spectators—we think these are not really our stories. But every once in a while God's Spirit intervenes and the stories deliver their intended jolt to our system: "*I'm* the ungrateful steward! This is *my* story!"

Jesus offers us "a gentle, listening language of suggestion, language that invites participation, language that doesn't say too much but leaves room for mystery."[10] Jesus offers us new frames—often quite paradoxical—through which we can see ourselves.

Reflection Questions

1. Can you believe that the person visibly acting out in a family might be doing so as part of a larger system in which every family member is a participant? Or have you ever been seen by others, or thought of yourself, as the identified patient (perhaps not in a family, but at work or in a relationship)?

2. How do you react to these biblical examples of Jesus' reframing? Can you think of other examples in the Gospels?

3. Many of Jesus' paradoxical stories and parables have lost their edge to reframe life for us, either because they are too familiar or because we don't understand what a radical reversal they were proposing in their original context. What might we do about this?

4. Do you remember a time when you were jolted by one of Jesus' stories, thinking, "That's *me* in the story!"

Chapter 7

TERROR AND TRUTH ON FLIGHT 451

Faith by itself, if it is not accompanied by action, is dead.
—James 2:17

It is by grace you have been saved, through faith—and this is not from yourselves, it is the gift of God—not by works, so that no one can boast.
—Ephesians 2:8–9

S he had finally dozed off on the long transatlantic flight to Frankfurt when it happened. As she leaned against her husband, who was sitting beside her in the aisle seat, her sleepy reverie of their long-awaited two-week tour of Europe was interrupted by a raspy voice coming over the speaker system. "This airplane has been commandeered by the Warriors of God. We are armed and have taken the flight crew into our custody." When they rolled to a stop on the runway, cars with flashing blue lights surrounded the plane. Through the window, she could see men in black—a German counterterrorist team maybe—crouched behind the cars. Again came the voice, cold as ice: "In twenty minutes this airplane will take off for an undisclosed location, where those remaining on board will be the guests of the Warriors of God.

While the airplane is being refueled, we will interview each passenger. All non-Christians will be allowed to exit the airplane before takeoff. If you cooperate fully, no one will be hurt."

The words exploded in her brain. "They only want Christians?" she thought. "Dear Jesus, how can this be happening to me?" Immediately two men in business suits, brandishing pistols, approached the couple in the first row. One of the men grabbed the woman's purse and began rummaging through it while his companion fired questions at them. "They're searching for evidence that they're Christians," she realized as she unclasped her own purse. Her fingers came across a folded bulletin from Sunday worship only the day before. As she surreptitiously hid the bulletin in the seat pocket in front of her, she was transported back to the worship service.

She was in the familiar sanctuary, half-listening to the sermon about the letter to Smyrna in the book of Revelation as she daydreamed about leaving for Europe the next day. The preacher was telling a story that came back to her now as she watched the men slowly moving down the aisle toward her. It was about a bishop of the early church at Smyrna in Asia Minor, named Polycarp, whom the preacher said was one of the earliest Christian martyrs. Polycarp refused to burn incense to the Roman emperor, an act of worship claiming the emperor as his divine Lord. A second-century document records that an officer urged Polycarp to reconsider. "What harm can it do to sacrifice to the emperor and be saved?" the officer asked. Polycarp refused. The old bishop was brought before the Roman proconsul in the amphitheater, who also pleaded with him. "Swear by the genius of Caesar and I will release you; revile the Christ." To which Polycarp replied, "Eighty-six years I have served him and he has done me no wrong; how then can I blaspheme my King who saved me?" When the crowds heard this, angry Jews and Romans gathered wood, and Polycarp was burned at the stake. With his last words, he thanked God that he was worthy to share the cup of Christ's suffering.

"How do you get that kind of courage?" she wanted to know. "Maybe if you're eighty-six, facing death is easier." Was she facing death now? The voice said they were merely taking hostages, but her mind flashed to pictures of lifeless bodies in other terrorist attacks. She could probably lie about her faith and pull it off. Since she was sitting in almost the last row, she'd spent the past minutes inconspicuously sanitizing her purse of any Christian symbols. Why claim to be a Christian when it very well might cause her death? She wouldn't mean the denials she'd give to these killers. God would understand. They were only words anyway. What other choice did she have?

She'd made lots of choices over the years. Suddenly, in one of those flashes of insight that sometimes comes in a crisis, she realized her choices had not prepared her for this moment.

When her friend Maxine was going through her divorce, she had thought about bringing Christ into their conversations. But she was sure Maxine would spread it all over town that she was some kind of fundamentalist religious fanatic; she never mentioned Jesus to Maxine. When her bridge group got into gossiping about others in their church, as they often did, sometimes she thought she should call them on it. But she'd spent years building these relationships; she didn't want to alienate her friends. Only a few months earlier, the pastor's sermon on giving had pricked her conscience about tithing their income. When she talked to her husband and he explained what areas would have to be cut back in their spending, she decided to drop it.

She knew she was a Christian. She knew that without her faith in Christ, she never could have coped when her mother died last year. Until this moment, she had just assumed that Christians in the modern world were never asked to prove their faith.

Her thoughts were snapped back to the present by the hysterical screams of a woman only three rows ahead. She was being dragged off the plane. Her husband remained behind after apparently confessing his faith in Christ. "Probably another Polycarp," she thought to herself, although he looked to be only about forty. Could she be that brave? She wondered. Her hand went to her neck, and she felt the gold cross necklace under her silk blouse. Her daughter had given it to her only the day before for her fortieth wedding anniversary. Ever so slowly, her hands crept around her neck until she could unclasp it and bring it down to her lap. She reached out to put it in the seat pocket in front of her, but she couldn't make herself let go of it. The cross symbolized far more than an anniversary gift. Her daughter had grown up in the church. Then, like many before her, she had drifted away and stopped attending. It was only now in her thirties, after the birth of her first child, that she had reconnected with Christ. The cross was a gift saying, "I'm back, Mom. I believe in Christ again, like you do." She couldn't part with the cross. She clenched it in her hand, thinking she could shove it into the seat cushions behind her if necessary.

Now that the men were only two rows in front of her, she saw something that horrified and revolted her. They required everyone who did not claim Jesus Christ to spit onto an image of his face before they left the airplane. With a passion for symbolism, apparently they assumed no true follower of Jesus could ever spit in his face. This was how they intended to separate Christians from non-Christians.

Now the men had reached her row and were talking to her husband. Her throat tightened; no sound came out. She thought of the choices she had made. The cost of following Jesus had been there all along: being labeled a fanatic if she talked about Jesus to Maxine, taking stands that might not be popular with her friends, giving her money sacrificially. But she had dodged them all. Now here she was, facing the greatest cost of all, and all she could do was stare at the face of Jesus held by the terrorist, with the repulsive saliva running down the Lord's cheeks. As she looked into that face, suddenly it appeared as though the saliva was transformed into tears—tears running down Jesus' face, *tears for her* . . . tears of love and understanding.

The dark, piercing eyes swung away from her husband and bored into her soul. The terrorist held the picture of Jesus toward her until it was only a few inches away from her face, so close that the saliva ran off the edges and dropped onto the new silk skirt she had bought for the trip. He snarled at her, "What about you?"

———————

I first preached this story/sermon on the faith/works paradox long ago, indeed about a decade before the 9/11 attacks. Solely a product of my imagination, it proved eerily prescient: in 2015 terrorist gunmen separated Christians from non-Christians when attacking a small college in Kenya.

As we have seen, many of Jesus' stories offer shocking, paradoxical choices that make us uncomfortable. Open-endedness pulls us into the story. We identify with characters and are vicariously forced to make our own choices. It is an error to draw points, lessons, or principles from Jesus' stories; too often we kill by dissection. Instead, we should seek the same dramatic impact they made on their original audience. Jesus' goal is never idle contemplation, but up-on-our-feet response. In discussing Jesus' storytelling, Eugene Peterson believes Jesus does not care much about telling abstract truths about God but rather "intends to get us involved, our feet in the mud and our hands in the bread dough, with the living God who is at work in this world. This is why Jesus tells stories, not to inform or explain or define, but to get us actively in on the ways and will of God in the homes and neighborhoods and workplaces where we spend our time."[1]

What will *we* do? How will *we* respond? This is where Jesus' stories (and my small example) want to take us. Most of us will, thankfully, never face the decision this woman does (spitting in Jesus' face is, perhaps, a twenty-first-century fictional parallel to Polycarp's burning incense to Caesar), but all of us face the issue in other ways. The stark choice has no soothing resolution and leaves the listener not with answers but rather a final question: "What about you?"

My story gets its bite from the perceived tension between Paul's clarion calls for faith apart from works (Eph. 2:8–9) and James's equally uncompromising claim that faith without works is dead (James 2:17). I say "perceived," because this tension is maintained only by defining faith and works contrary to their contexts. When Paul speaks of works, he highlights Christian faith against the background of ritualized works-righteousness. James, on the other hand, speaks of faith as mental agreement; for James, faith without works reveals inadequate faith, for genuine faith means a changed life. Because we in the global north tend to conceptualize faith as mental agreement, we find ourselves wrestling with this presumed paradox far more than do our brothers and sisters in the global south, whose cultures naturally assume that faith requires showing public allegiance and inevitably leads to action.

As with all the playful paradoxes we have been considering, the tension between faith and works can thus ultimately be resolved. However, realizing that faith and works are not contradictory does not forfeit the paradox's ability to capture our attention and reframe reality. Pitting faith against works forces us to reflect on the nature of faith in our lives: how integrated is our faith with our behavior, especially when put to the test? As in Jesus' use of paradox, the story of Flight 451 invites us to connect the dots for ourselves.

Reflection Questions

1. If you were the woman in the story, what do you imagine you would do?

2. Have you ever had to make a public identification with Jesus that carried negative consequences (perhaps with family, friends, or colleagues)?

3. What kind of small decisions are you making every day that might prepare you if you are ever on "Flight 451"?

4. Has faith versus works been an issue in your life so far?

Chapter 8

PAVLOV'S DOGS

*The test of a first-rate intelligence is the ability to hold two
opposed ideas in the mind at the same time and still retain
the ability to function.*

—F. Scott Fitzgerald

In 1927, Russian psychologist I. P. Pavlov began an experiment using
his soon-to-be-famous dogs. This was not his celebrated conditioned-
response experiment, in which dogs salivated at the sound of their food
bell. Rather, Pavlov showed a dog the figure of a circle, then immediately fed the dog. When the dog was conditioned to expect food each
time it saw the circle, Pavlov varied the routine by showing the dog
an ellipse, which was not rewarded. The dog soon learned to choose
the circle over the ellipse to obtain his food. Pavlov then did something mildly diabolical. He slowly made the ellipse more and more
circular, until the dog could no longer tell the difference between the
circle and the almost-circular ellipse. Now the dog squealed, wiggled
about, barked at experimenters, and became generally unruly. Pavlov
called this result "experimental neurosis"—a subject becomes neurotic
if placed in a highly ambiguous situation in which choosing the correct
response is impossible.

Since Pavlov's day, much attention has focused on subjects immobilized in highly confusing or paradoxical situations called "double
binds." A double bind has three distinguishing characteristics.[1] First,
the subject must be in a relationship that includes a high degree of

psychological and/or physical survival value. Husband/wife, parent/child, employer/employee, counselor/client, and close friendships are all examples.

Second, within this relationship, the subject faces a paradoxical directive that is impossible to fulfill. Thus the classic Jewish mother joke: "Give your son Marvin two sports shirts as a present. The first time he wears one, look at him sadly and say in your Basic Tone of Voice: 'The other one you didn't like?'"[2] Obviously, there is no way out! Whichever shirt Marvin wears will always disappoint his mother! Such is the nature of double binds.

Third, in a double bind, the subject can neither withdraw from the relationship nor question the meaning or appropriateness of the paradoxical directive. If we could just step outside the situation and discuss it with the other person (Marvin telling his mother that wearing one shirt does not mean he does not like the other one), we would slip out of the bind. But the double bind never allows this honest reflection or discussion.

Caught in Painful Double Binds

When does paradox cease being playful and instead become painful? We have seen how Jesus employs paradoxical tension to promote second-order change—for example, reframing issues in ways that push his listeners beyond accustomed worldviews. In all these cases, the paradoxical tension between seeming opposites is resolved when the paradox has done its work. But what if we cannot reflect or discuss? Then the tension is never resolved, and the paradox can become a double bind.

Look at the three characteristics of double binds in a Christian context. First, there is definitely a psychological, emotional, or existential stake in our relationship with God. Second, someone representing God (not God) gives us a command that seems impossible to perform, as when Pavlov's dogs were required to choose between the circle and the almost-circular ellipse. Third, this same someone representing God (not God) tells us we are not allowed to question the command, reflect on it, or even discuss it with others; to question the command is to question God.

For example, the Bible says, "Rejoice in the Lord always" (Phil. 4:4). We are advised this means feeling perpetually joyful; we are further advised that not feeling perpetually joyful is a poor witness to non-believers and suggests something is lacking in our spiritual maturity. On the other hand, it is impossible to maintain any emotional state for long (whether joy or anything else). This inevitably leads some earnest Christians into a double bind—willing oneself to appear joyful on the outside, while (at times) feeling anything but joyful on the inside. Since emotions rarely bow to will, this failure of willpower often leads to guilt, anxiety, or depression—all opposites of joy!

Are all negative emotions unspiritual? Is perpetual joy the only measure of a person's spirituality? I watch a widow in the back row silently crying through every song. She tells me after the service, "When I come to worship, I'm so embarrassed. All I do is sit and cry!" I tell her that it's okay to come to worship and cry. In fact, what better place could God meet her in her sorrow than in worship? (See Ps. 34:18.)

The way out of all double binds is to disobey the third requirement, to question whether the directive (for example, a person must always feel joyful) is legitimate. In this case, we have much biblical evidence that it is not. The Psalms at times throb with grief and despair, and a whole book in the Bible is called Lamentations. What about Jesus expressing sorrow and dread in Gethsemane (Matt. 26:36–46)? Often believers approach God weeping and wearing sackcloth and ashes (Neh. 8:9; Job 42:6; Lam. 2:5, 10; Dan. 9:3; John 11:33). In fact, God wants his people to lament (Zech. 12:10–14; Rom. 12:15)! Why, we might ask, do we not worship God as the psalmists do, with our full range of human emotions? Perhaps the answer is pragmatic: how do we justify a "downer" service to people expecting to leave worship every week feeling uplifted? A growing number of churches in America no longer celebrate Good Friday (or even Lent) because they cannot imagine worship encompassing sober lament.

The false assumption that God promises Christians protection from suffering sets up another classic double bind. In this scenario, suffering becomes evidence of distance from God. If God is not blessing you, if your loved one dies, if you have unmet needs, if you are depressed, anxious, despairing, if you express any kind of human weakness, you must lack faith. Such is the cancer of the prosperity gospel, currently metastasizing in many corners of the Christian world today.

Double binds can become truly oppressive. I suspect that countless Christians caught in toxic double binds suffer in silence, too embarrassed to admit such spiritual "failure." Indeed, just like Pavlov's dogs, Christians can exhibit an induced neurosis, with symptoms ranging from depression, anxiety, excessive feelings of guilt, and stress-related somatic problems to more serious disorientation and even psychotic reactions.[3]

A Way Out?

Paradox in Jesus' hands is playfully therapeutic; it reframes reality in life-giving ways. Now we have seen a shadow side: double binds that even induce neurosis, as in Pavlov's dogs. Tragically, I have known people to reject Christ or turn away from his church when they witness such emotional entrapment in friends, family, or themselves. More tragic, sometimes the church itself sets up the impossible directives that create the double binds, and then brooks no arguments or questions.

We can help each other avoid debilitating double binds by reflecting openly, especially about paradox. Double binds happen in the first place, remember, because we cannot question or discuss the ways we feel caught. Raising paradoxical biblical issues as legitimate inquiries, as Cheryl did (see chap. 1), allows us to consider whether the paradox is real or only a double bind resulting from misreading or misapplication of Scripture.

But, just as in Jesus' use of paradox, might some double binds be therapeutic? I believe so, but only if they are ones God allows rather than ones that result from a misuse of Scripture imposed by religious leaders or churches. Saul, who becomes the apostle Paul, provides the classic example. On the Damascus Road, when Jesus says, "It is hard for you to kick against the goads" (Acts 26:14), he implies that Saul's refusal to consider Jesus' way is hurting Saul. A goad is a sharp stick farmers use to prod stubborn oxen into motion. The more the animal kicks against it, the deeper it penetrates into the animal's flesh. It is much better for the ox to obey the will of its master. Painful double binds can be therapeutic if they goad us outside our systems to a second-order solution. Much later, Paul reflects that the harder he tried to be righteous before God, the farther from God his effort took him (Phil. 3:3–9). "Only by being placed in this therapeutic double bind was Paul able to make the conceptual shift from one system to another totally different, even paradoxical one in which righteousness comes not by work, but by faith in Christ."[4]

These try-harder double binds can, as with Paul, open us to God's grace. They show us we can never try hard enough. I suspect the Lord allowed me (and others like me) to suffer through my own try-harder issues for just this reason. When caught in the Chinese handcuffs, we discover new depths in a God able to do in and for us what we can never do in and for ourselves. "My grace is sufficient for you, for my power is made perfect in weakness" (2 Cor. 12:9). Therapeutic indeed.

Reflection Questions

1. Have you ever found yourself caught in a double bind? What was it?

2. Do you agree that Christians might be especially susceptible to such double binds? Have you seen any examples in your experience?

3. Do you think the author is going too far in suggesting that some paradoxical double binds might be therapeutic?

4. Are there certain conditions that might make some double binds therapeutic for Christians, while other double binds will never have any redeeming qualities?

PART 3

THE TUNING FORK

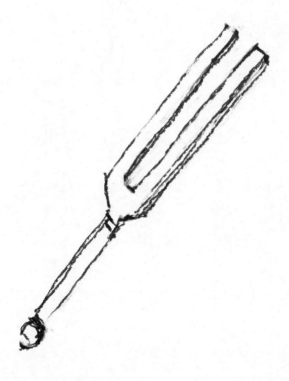

Chapter 9

THE TUNING FORK

*An opposite can agree with its opposite, but even more
beautiful is the harmony of discordances.*

—Heraclitus, Fragment 8

Lucy Maud Montgomery is best known for writing the popular Anne
of Green Gables novels, which were set in the sharp beauty of turn-
of-the-century Prince Edward Island. Mark Twain called them the
sweetest creation of child life yet written. Less well known is another
series of novels Montgomery wrote with a different heroine. In the first
book of that series, *Emily of the New Moon*, Emily discovers mysteries
lurking beneath the ordinary world around her, as in these evocative
lines: "[S]he could never draw the curtain aside—but sometimes, just
for a moment, a wind fluttered it and then it was as if she caught a
glimpse of the enchanting realm beyond—only a glimpse—and heard
the note of unearthly music."[1] Listen as Emily describes this unearthly
note, and see if it does not raise some glimmers in your memory, as it
does in mine: "This moment came rarely—went swiftly, leaving her
breathless with the inexpressible delight of it. Tonight the dark boughs
against that far off sky had given it. It had come with a high, wild note
of wind in the night, with a shadow wave over a ripe field, with a gray
bird lighting on her windowsill in a storm, with the singing of 'Holy!
Holy! Holy!' in church, with the glimpse of the kitchen fire when she
had come home on a dark autumn night, with the spirit-like blue of

ice palms on a twilight pane, with a felicitous new word when she was writing down a 'description' of something. And always when the flash came to her Emily felt that life was a wonderful, mysterious thing of persistent beauty."[2]

How might these moments, or notes, of inexpressibly mysterious beauty be heard in Scripture? Consider a tuning fork. To ring true, a tuning fork must be carefully held. Dampen either tine with your fingers, even a little, and the note disappears. Neither tine by itself can produce the sweet, pure note. A tuning fork delivers a true pitch only when both tines vibrate together.

In this section, I want to explore how some biblical paradoxes declare their truthful note through contrasting poles vibrating in unison. In this order of paradox, two contrasting ideas create their paradoxical tension in the space between them. Each side offers part of the truth (and none of the truth when considered in isolation). Neither side can be muffled, even a little, if the sweet, pure note of unearthly music is to be heard. Listening for this note requires care and honesty. Unlike a tuning fork forged of metal, these paradoxes of Scripture are forged of *words*: two disparate ideas put side by side until they vibrate together as one. Words are hard to manage, especially when we bring our own dispositions and biases that put a slightly greater stress on one side or the other, muffling the note.

Balance or Tension?

As we imagine the relationship created by these contrasting poles of a paradox, we might think of compromise. But we are not dealing with each side altering its agenda just enough to find middle ground. Neither does Aristotle's "golden mean" apply, for the same reason: each side of the paradox must remain at 100 percent strength if the truth is to be heard.

Perhaps our image should be a precariously balanced circus rider, each foot planted on one of two horses thundering side by side around center ring. A drawback of balance, however, is that it implies that, with enough practice, we might keep everything under control. Think of riding a bike: we begin to fall to one side, correct ourselves, begin to fall to the other side, correct ourselves again. If the handlebars were suddenly welded into a straight-ahead position, we would quickly fall; we could no longer make the small corrections necessary to keep our balance. (This is why street performers doing tricks on stationary bikes exhibit extraordinary balance. It's hard to avoid falling if you're not moving.) If keeping our balance in such a simple activity as biking is more complicated than we assume, what must keeping our balance in our relationship with God require? Do we always (even usually) sense the balancing corrections we need to make as we relate to God? It's possible some of us do. As for me, I usually sense a correction is needed only when the ground is fast rising toward me!

I suggest tension is a better image for understanding paradox. First, it is the tension between two seemingly opposite ideas that creates the paradox in the first place; remove the tension and the paradox evaporates, as we saw with many of Jesus' paradoxical sayings. Second, living within tension is often how a relationship actually feels. I do not mean tension in the sense of feeling anxious or emotionally vulnerable, as if constantly walking on eggshells. I have in mind a positive, life-giving tension, such as marriage partners feel living within the tension of both serving and being served by the other, or two good friends feel living within the tension of each sharing his or her own concerns while also focusing on the other's concerns. Losing such healthy tensions is usually detrimental to relationships.

Healthy tension is required in stringed instruments. Before a concert, the concertmaster plays a note on her violin, and all the string players tune their instruments by making small adjustments, tightening or loosening each string to achieve exactly the right tension. They become "in tune" with one another; such healthy tension produces great art.

C . . . ar

I was at a documentary film festival listening to mountaineer and film-maker Jimmy Chin describe his film *Meru* and what it is like to make one of the most difficult mountain climbs in the world. He mentioned paradox, and my ears pricked up. Facing a mountain that is almost impossible to climb (and on which many had previously failed or died) is terrifying, he said. At the same time, he went on, it is inspiring; there is a depth of human friendship and mutual dependence within the climbing team that few people ever experience.[3]

Rudolf Otto, in his classic *The Idea of the Holy*, identifies the numinous quality of the Holy as the tension of such opposites. There is the *mysterium tremendum*, a daunting sense of the "wholly other" which evokes feelings of awe and terror. In tension with the *mysterium tremendum* is the *fascinans*, an attractive, almost magnetic appeal that the numinous also exerts on us. "These two qualities," Otto suggests, "the daunting and the fascinating, now combine in a strange harmony of contrasts to flesh out our experience of the Holy."[4] Otto's description of a *strange harmony of contrasts* is what I am after. Just as Otto believes that terror and attraction can harmonize to produce a sense of the Holy, so we find in Scripture opposites harmonizing to produce larger truths.

The two-headed monster my kids used to watch on *Sesame Street* uses exactly this strategy. One head of the monster says, "C . . ." After two seconds, the other head says, "Ar." They look at one another, smile and nod, then do it again and again, each time with a shorter time interval between them: "C . . . ar," "C . . ar," "Car!" Two sounds that began separately meld together until one new word is heard; two ideas that began separately meld together until one new note of truth is heard.

Oxford theologian Paul Fiddes offers an evocative description of this tuning fork order of paradox when describing the music of poetry compared with prose: "By bringing two verbal signs together in an image, new levels of meaning are given to both. Between the objects compared there is *room for vibrations of undertones and overtones*; something altogether new happens which cannot be paraphrased in prose" (emphasis added).[5] Fiddes goes on to assert about these poetic vibrations,

"In their juxtaposition or 'interaction,' many relationships are evoked that need not be, or cannot be, expressed."[6] Just so, the paradoxes considered in this section function just this way, creating vibrations that evoke meanings and relationships that cannot be expressed directly.

Charles Simeon, a nineteenth-century English evangelical preacher, appreciated that the vastness of biblical truth could never be encapsulated, stating, "I soon learned that I must take the Scriptures with the simplicity of a little child, and be content to receive as God's testimony what he has revealed, whether I can unravel all the difficulties that may attend it or not."[7] He retained enviable freshness throughout fifty years of preaching, largely by remaining stubbornly independent of all the "isms" of his day and refusing to pigeonhole his theology. Simeon believed that apparently-opposed biblical truths served the larger purposes of God, just as wheels in a machine may move in opposite directions and yet serve a common end.[8] He defends his method of unequivocally preaching both sides of biblical paradox, even though advocates of this or that theological system might condemn him as inconsistent: "It is better to state these apparently opposite truths in the plain and unsophisticated manner of the Scriptures. . . . [I]f he speak in exact conformity with the Scriptures, he shall rest the vindication of his conduct simply on the authority and example of the Inspired Writers. He has no desire to be wise above what is written, nor any conceit that he can teach the Apostles to speak with more propriety and correctness than they have spoken."[9]

If contrasting biblical ideas present us with paradox, we must not file away their rough edges until we can somehow "harmonize" them. Instead, we can present both as clearly and distinctly as possible, then listen for the mysterious harmonious note they create together. We now investigate some of these paradoxes that invite us to place our faith, beyond human theological systems, in a mysterious God who is infinitely greater than any system.

Reflection Questions

1. Rudolf Otto suggests that our experience of the Holy is born in the contrasting harmony of "awe/terror" and "fascination/ attraction." Have you ever felt simultaneously terrified of and attracted to God? What was it like?

2. The tuning fork is used as a metaphor for two opposing scriptural ideas or principles vibrating together, like divine sovereignty and human responsibility. Can you think of other pairings of seemingly opposite truths in the Bible that might vibrate together this way?

3. Have two biblical ideas ever melded together in your mind, like *Sesame Street*'s "C . . . ar," "C . . ar," "Car"?

4. What might be the consequences of imposing our own harmony over opposing biblical truths, rather than patiently listening for the harmonious note these opposites might create when both are equally accepted?

Chapter 10

'COURSE HE ISN'T SAFE... BUT HE'S GOOD

God is the only comfort—he is also the supreme terror. The thing we most need and the thing we most want to hide from.
—C. S. Lewis, *Mere Christianity*

In C. S. Lewis's *The Lion, the Witch, and the Wardrobe*, Lucy and Susan are sheltered by Mr. and Mrs. Beaver, who tell them about Aslan, the great Lion who is the ruler of Narnia and the son of the Emperor-Beyond-the-Sea. Aslan, of course, is Lewis's figure for Jesus Christ. Let's listen in on their conversation:

> "Ooh!" said Susan, "I'd thought he was a man. Is he—quite safe? I shall feel rather nervous about meeting a lion."
>
> "That you will, dearie, and no mistake," said Mrs. Beaver, "if there's anyone who can appear before Aslan without their knees knocking, they're either braver than most or else just silly."
>
> "Then he isn't safe?" said Lucy.
>
> "Safe?" said Mr. Beaver. "Don't you hear what Mrs. Beaver tells you? Who said anything about safe? 'Course he isn't safe. But he's good."[1]

Mr. Beaver puts his paw on the first tuning fork–style paradox we will consider: God isn't safe, but God is good. As with all biblical paradoxes, living within this tension is difficult and yet essential. According to A. W. Tozer, the God we envision determines the person we are becoming: "We tend by a secret law of the soul to move toward our mental image of God." He continues, "Were we able to extract from any man a complete answer to the question, 'What comes into your mind when you think about God?' we might predict with certainty the spiritual future of that man."[2]

What happens to people who are primarily focused on a God who "isn't safe," or what the Bible speaks of as justice, judgment, or wrath? We already know. Those with the primary image of a wrathful God eventually become wrathful themselves. Those who believe only in a judging God easily become judgmental. Those who see God solely pursuing justice might end up like Inspector Javert in *Les Misérables*, a man so tragically consumed with exacting justice that he is unable to offer any mercy and, just as tragically, unable to receive mercy himself. None of these is a pretty picture of God, and folks who see God only in these ways are not endearing to be around. Since these judgmental caricatures are usually how Christians are portrayed in our media, who can blame churches for treating this unsafe God the way families deal with odd Uncle Harry: keep him in the background so he doesn't embarrass us in front of the guests.

What about the other side of Mr. Beaver's statement: "He's good"? Even beyond good, doesn't the Bible say, "God is love"? Unfortunately, we can subtly turn that biblical statement on its head until it becomes, "Love is God." We then fall prey to the opposite caricature: God the benignly loving heavenly grandfather, who smiles on his children no matter what they do. If this is our mental image of God, we easily assume that any loving person is automatically a godly person or that any belief system with some love in it must also have God in it. Experience shows that neither is true. Though most of us are more familiar with the first caricature, I wonder if this second is not, in the end, more damaging. God is not *only* loving; God is also just. In fact, if God were not perfect justice, neither could God be perfect love.

Two Gods?

The biblical writers speak of God's judgment often and without embarrassment. God judged Adam and Eve and expelled them from the garden. God's judgment destroyed the world with a flood at the time of Noah. God judged the Egyptians with ten plagues before the exodus of Israel. God judged the Israelites who worshiped the golden calf in the wilderness, and they perished. God judged the nations of Israel and Judah when they worshiped other gods: Assyria conquered Israel, the Babylonians laid waste to Judah, and the famous ten lost tribes were never heard from again. God is not embarrassed to claim this judgment: "I form the light and create darkness, I bring prosperity and create disaster; I, the Lord, do all these things" (Isa. 45:7).

Some people think this Old Testament God of justice is just a warm-up act, preparing the audience for the real God of love to take the stage in the New Testament. The God of judgment steps aside while snare drums roll and an announcer's silky voice booms out: "Now that you're thoroughly frightened and feeling convicted . . . here's the God you've *all* been waiting for . . . all the way to you from Bethlehem and Nazareth . . . the God who *reeeaaalllly* loves you . . . Jeeessssus Chriiiissssst!"

Yet no new God appears onstage. There is only one God. God's enduring love is on display throughout the Old Testament: "Because of the Lord's great love we are not consumed, for his compassions never fail" (Lam. 3:22). God lifts the yoke of Egyptian slavery from Israel and time and again fulfills his covenant promises even though his people forsake theirs.

Neither is God's justice forgotten in the New Testament. As the incarnation of a loving God, Jesus spends an embarrassing amount of time talking about judgment. Many of his parables end with people being "thrown outside, into the darkness, where there will be weeping and gnashing of teeth" (Matt. 8:12). Justice is actually heightened in the New Testament, because the New Testament clearly looks forward to a final day of judgment: "Then I saw a great white throne and him who was seated on it. The earth and the heavens fled from his presence, and there was no place for them. And I saw the dead, great and small, standing before the throne, and books were opened. Another book was opened, which is the book of life. The dead were judged according to what they had done as recorded in the books" (Rev. 20:11–12). And who does the judging? Jesus says, "The Father judges no one, *but has entrusted all judgment to the Son*" (John 5:22, emphasis added).

A. W. Tozer writes, "The vague and tenuous hope that God is too kind to punish the ungodly has become a deadly opiate for the consciences of millions."[3] An opiate is a drug that dulls our senses, makes us lose touch with reality. It's a fatal notion that a loving God could never judge anyone. Why do we assume that love and justice do not coexist in God? C. S. Lewis says with wonderful understatement, "Some people talk as if meeting the gaze of absolute goodness would be fun. They need to think again."[4] God is so good, God's love is so pure, that nothing impure can stand before him. It's the justice of God that shows us what terrible trouble we're in, that makes us feel the heavy weight of wrongdoing that Christian in *The Pilgrim's Progress* carries on his back. It's the love of God, through Jesus Christ's sacrificial death on the cross, that allows Christian's burden of sin to be released.

An Intolerable Compliment

Some of the most heart-wrenching counseling sessions I've had over the years have been with parents wrestling with how to be both loving and just with their children. Often the issue is substance abuse. A child steals from his or her parents to support a habit. "How can I kick my child out into the street?" these parents ask. "How can I see my child go to jail?" It was through such anguishing situations that "tough love" entered our vocabulary in the 1980s. We realized that sometimes love needs to be tough. Genuine love must be tough enough to allow loved ones to suffer the consequences of their actions.

In a far deeper way, God's love is a tough love. The author of Hebrews proclaims, "Have you completely forgotten this word of encouragement that addresses you as a father addresses his son? It says,

'My son, do not make light of the Lord's discipline, and do not lose heart when he rebukes you, because the Lord disciplines the one he loves, and he chastens everyone he accepts as his son'" (Heb. 12:5–6). Neither does God's love cancel out clear teachings of the Bible that might not seem loving from our perspective (for example, the reality of hell). In *The Problem of Pain*, C. S. Lewis says that God has paid us the "intolerable compliment" of loving us. Those two words, *intolerable* and *compliment*, are not often used together. What is an intolerable compliment?

Imagine an artist who loves a painting, the greatest work of her life. The artist lavishes it with care and often scrapes off the paint and starts certain sections over until she paints them just right. If the painting could talk, after being scraped and started over for the tenth time, it might say it would rather be a quick thumbnail sketch than endure all this revision. We might also wish that God cared less about what he is creating in our lives. But if we wish that God cared less about the person we are becoming, we are asking not for more love but for less. C. S. Lewis expands this idea: "Those Divine demands which sound to our natural ears most like those of a despot and least like those of a lover, in fact marshal us where we should want to go if we knew what we wanted. That is, whether we like it or not, God intends to give us what we need, not what we now think we want. Once more, we are embarrassed by the intolerable compliment, by too much love, not too little."[5]

C. S. Lewis is saying, "You asked for a loving God, people. Well, you have one!" God's love is all the more magnificent because it includes perfect justice. And this tough inner fiber of justice is what makes it perfect love! It is all a mystery we will never comprehend. But like *Sesame Street*'s two-headed monster whose "C . . ." and ". . . Ar" harmonize to become "Car," so Mr. Beaver: "'Course he isn't safe. But he's good."

Reflection Questions

1. Do you agree with A. W. Tozer that we "tend by a secret law of the soul to move toward our mental image of God"? What evidence have you seen for this?

2. Which side of the paradox do you gravitate toward, a loving God or a just God? How about most of the Christians you know?

3. Does C. S. Lewis's metaphor of God's love as an "intolerable compliment" change your view of the love of God? Explain.

4. When we choose not to live within the paradoxical tension created by God's love and God's judgment, what consequences have you observed in personal, family, or church life?

Chapter 11

NOW MY EYES SEE

The loss of mystery has led to a loss of majesty. The more we know, the less we believe. No wonder there is no wonder.
—Max Lucado, *In the Grip of Grace*

Job offers a vivid example of how harmonious paradox opens a door into the mystery of God. Job has lost everything. Sitting in a comfortable chair reading Job's story hardly prepares us to relate to the cascading, cataclysmic loss of Job's loved ones, his material well-being, his health—everything. To figuratively sit with Job as he scrapes his sores with a potsherd (Job 2:8), we might need to sit with the Ethiopian women my wife sat with every week, women who sorted through mountains of stinking garbage in Addis Ababa every day to stay alive. They ask along with Job, Is God aloof from my pain? Has God forgotten me? Or does God still have his eye on me, even here, even now? Many of us have asked this question: how is this all-powerful, high-and-lifted-up God still personally involved in the yawning depths of my trials? As we track Job's conversations with his friends and with God, however, Job allows both tines of the tuning fork (God high and God low) to keep vibrating.

At the end of his story, Job rejects all simple solutions. God's ways are mysterious and unsearchable; who is Job to discern or judge them? "And these are but the outer fringe of his works; how faint the whisper we hear of him! Who then can understand the thunder of his power?"

(Job 26:14). Acknowledging he stands before mystery, Job declares, "Surely I spoke of things I did not understand, things too wonderful for me to know" (Job 42:3). Yet living in this paradox—a God so high above him and yet still with him—has clarified for Job a crucial truth: his faith must be in God, not in what he knows about God.

A woman in our congregation lost her husband to cancer and was left with two young children to raise by herself. As we walked together over several months through various stages of grief, she repeatedly wished for a sign that God still cared for her. Periodically she would say, "If God does this for me, maybe I can trust him again." The signs never came. God always failed her tests. To her credit, she described God's failures not in angry, derisive tones but with a piquant longing for an assurance of God's presence, which she thought she had lost forever. "Why can't God just do this one simple thing for me to show me he's still there?" she often lamented. In theological language, she believed that God was transcendent (far beyond her), but she had lost confidence that God was also immanent (involved in her personal life).

During one of our conversations, she offhandedly described how several mundane issues had gone unexpectedly well for her. In one of those moments when the words came out without a lot of forethought, I replied, "Maybe God has given you the signs you wanted all along." I asked her which showed her own love toward her children: giving in when they jumped up and down clamoring for a treat, or caring for their needs through a multitude of unrecognized but essential chores day in and day out? Suddenly something changed. Through new eyes, together we began identifying signs of God's love during her tragic loss and its aftermath. New insights started to flow. Perhaps God had indeed been involved in her life all along.

Stars and Sparrows

God is *transcendent*. God is not part of creation, not even the highest or best part, for as its Creator, God surpasses our universe and is not bound by space and time as we are. One of our most basic Christian beliefs (although we rarely think about it) is that God is ontologically different from creation—different in essence or being. (*Ontological* comes from the Greek word *ontos* for "being.") Diogenes Allen reminds us that when we distinguish between a real duck and a duck decoy as both float on a pond, we are making an ontological distinction. Living flesh and carved wood are different in essence or being. In a far more radical way, the reality of creation and the reality of God are utterly distinct—so distinct that we creatures do not even have mental categories to express the difference between our Creator and ourselves.[1]

This ontological difference is the reason why God always remains a mystery to us—in fact, we could know nothing whatever of God (any more than the wooden duck can know anything of the living duck) had God not graciously chosen to reveal himself to us through creation, through Scripture, and most fully in Jesus Christ. Thus the mystery of God is not just one theological idea to be set alongside many others; mystery is part of *every* doctrine about God. The first Soviet cosmonaut returned to earth thinking he had struck a fatal blow to Christianity when he announced he had surveyed the heavens but had not seen God. Of course he hadn't. God is transcendent.

God is also *immanent*. God is a personal being actively engaged in the creation, so that we, who are also personal beings and are created in God's image, can have a relationship with our Creator. Moreover, the Bible gives several hints that God is so personally involved in the creation that the divine power keeps it intact, perhaps even at the subatomic level: "He is before all things, and in him all things hold together" (Col. 1:17).

Scripture paints beautiful pictures of both sides of this paradox. Our sun is one of a billion stars in the Milky Way galaxy, which is one of a billion galaxies (see Gen. 1:14–19). Our vast universe gives clues to the grandeur of its Creator, yet God transcends even the universe itself; God is not part of the universe and existed before it came to be. Carl Sagan, while no friend of Christianity, identified how we diminish God's transcendence in his 1985 Gifford Lectures: "A general problem with much of Western theology in my view is that the God portrayed is too small. It is a god of a tiny world and not a god of a galaxy, much less a universe."[2]

On the other hand, God is so personally involved in our lives that he provides for our daily needs as he does for the sparrows (Matt. 10:29, 31). God knows us through and through (Ps. 139). Even the hairs on our heads are numbered (Matt. 10:30). Perhaps we see the personal nature of God in no better place than garden-variety prayer: that such a transcendent Being would enter into dialogue with us poor creatures is truly astounding! Commenting on the intersection of the transcendent and immanent, William Alston writes, "Our understanding of prayer is one of the prime loci of the pervasive tension in Christian thought between God as 'wholly other' and God as a partner in interpersonal relationships."[3]

Two Dangers

In *A History of God*, Karen Armstrong observes that the God we meet in the Old Testament is a "tribal deity Yahweh [who] was murderously partial to his own people."[4] She suggests that "the idea of a personal God seems increasingly unacceptable at the present time for all kinds of reasons: moral, intellectual, scientific and spiritual,"[5] and we should instead "seek to find a 'God' above this personal God," a God who is "beyond personality."[6] She goes on, "Ever since biblical times, theists had been aware of the paradoxical nature of the God to which they prayed, aware that the personalized God was balanced by the essentially transpersonal divinity."[7] Armstrong believes that this paradox no longer holds. Crippled by aimlessness and alienation, many find that a personal God "no longer works for them."[8] All that remains, then, is the transcendent or transpersonal side of the paradox: "This God is to be approached through the imagination and can be seen as a kind of art form, akin to the other great artistic symbols that have expressed the ineffable mystery, beauty, and value of life."[9]

Many themes of the liberal theological tradition are present in this statement: affinity for subjective experience, sensitivity to mystery, imaginative openness that assumes God's reality can never be locked into human concepts, and especially, a desire to be in tune with contemporary culture. That modern people hunger for mystery in just these ways shows how in tune Armstrong is with her audience. Twentieth-century examples include Paul Tillich's notion of God as Ground of Being who "was not a distinct state with a name of its own but pervaded each one of our normal human experiences,"[10] or Pierre Teilhard de Chardin's vision of God as a divine force driving the evolutionary process. But when we jettison a personal God to satisfy our cultural expectations, are we not in danger of actually losing the God we meet in the pages of Scripture?

Others, of course, are repelled by the very notion of God as "a kind of art form." Generally suspicious of mystery, this group prefers to tell it like it is—no intellectual qualifications, no wishy-washiness, no indecision. The message here seems to be that Christian faith is one place where everything can still be spelled out. How reassuring to modern people anxious to make sense of their fast-changing world. The truth is captured—pinned down like a butterfly—ready for closer inspection. In significant ways, this mindset is *also* in tune with American culture—the segments that yearn for security, simplicity, and solid answers in the face of change.

But to this group I want to ask, Can every truth of Scripture be captured and mounted so easily? Do not some biblical truths elude us, beautifully intriguing and sun-dappled with color, yet fluttering just beyond our rational grasp? Can all biblical truth be reduced to bullet points? Can the truths of the Bible be spoon-fed to us, or do they occasionally require a good deal of gnawing? Is it not also telling it like it is to declare that this mysterious Holy Other is far beyond our comprehension? Here is the opposite danger: God becomes trivialized, shrunken to meet human needs—as a supernatural vending machine, as everyone's buddy, or as a symbol of American civil religion.[11] To sum up, taking only one side of this paradoxical God ends up either in relativism (everything about God is a matter of my interpretation and preferences) or in dogmatism (everything about God is known and possessed by me); neither is congenial to some of us.

Tension Again

How do we relate to a God who is simultaneously transcendent and immanent, ontologically different from all creation yet personally involved in that creation? My friend grieving her husband had lost this tension. Still aware of God's transcendence, she questioned whether God was personally involved in her life. One of the qualities of mystery is that it reveals even as it hides. Seeking a sign that God was still with her in her loss, this woman discovered God unexpectedly present in the ordinary routines of life. God revealed even as God hid.

At the end of his wrestling with God, Job admits that God is unfathomable, but Job also (paradoxically) indicates that he now knows God better than he did before. "My ears had heard of you but now my eyes have seen you" (Job 42:5). Intriguingly, Job's last word on the subject is not "I understand" or "I believe" but rather "I repent" (see Job 42:6). Perhaps he repents of his inadequate vision of God, which this encounter has exploded. Might some of us also say "I repent" as we discover that God is far more transcendent, or far more personal, than we have always assumed?

Why is seeking to live in this tension important? Why not simply gravitate toward whichever pole of the paradox is more personally attractive to us (God high or God low)? What happens, for example, if we focus only on a low, immanent God? Surely a God who knows us so well that even the hairs on our head are numbered is a great personal comfort, especially during hard times. Yet when we embrace only God's immanence, we end up with a heavenly buddy who likes hanging out with us but, as our Best Friend, asks very little of us. Here we might also mention some approaches to worship (or worship music) that are criticized for dumbing down God's transcendence.

On the other hand, what happens when we focus only on a high, transcendent God? We might end up as the eighteenth-century deists, whose God was so high that God was AWOL from human life entirely, the famous watchmaker God who set the universe ticking but then disappeared to parts unknown. Deism and its modern equivalents quickly degenerate into humanism; adherents try to follow the natural law or ethical principles God has left behind, but only through their human ability. For some people who have trouble with the supernatural (seen throughout the biblical record and undergirding Christian faith in general), such a high but very distant God is just the ticket—we are left with some principles to follow, but we're on our own.

When we do not keep the high and low in constant tension, we risk accepting a caricature of God; we miss the pure note of truth heard only when the transcendent and immanent vibrate together in unison.

Reflection Questions

1. Can you think of any personal experience, like the woman's in the opening story in this chapter, where you lost contact with either God's transcendence beyond you or God's personal involvement with you?

2. Which danger do you find more prominent for you: so neglecting God's immanence that God becomes "a kind of art form" or so forgetting God's transcendence that God becomes your buddy?

3. Which of the dangers in question 2 do you think is more common in your church community or among Christians you might know? Why do you think this might be so?

4. After reading this chapter, is your response similar to Job's "I repent," or something else?

Chapter 12

WHO CHOOSES FIRST?

The Scriptures . . . accurately reflect the real world in which we live, and most of us are so well acquainted with paradox and perplexity in our own experience that we understand. Only the arrogant and the dogmatic find paradox hard to accept.

—Richard Foster, *Money, Sex, and Power*

When I do premarital counseling, one of my standard initial questions for the couple is, "When did you know he or she was the right one?" Couples often have fun disagreeing about who took the initiative in the relationship. One person will say, "I chose you." Then the other will say, "That's what I *wanted* you to think. But I really chose you." Everyone laughs. It makes little difference on their wedding day who chose first. When it comes to a relationship with God, however, the paradox of divine sovereignty and human free will—does God choose first or do we?—creates an uncomfortable tension at the very center of Christian life.

Does my salvation depend on God's sovereign choice of me (often called election) or my response to the gospel message (human free will)? Does God's choice of me predetermine my choice for God? Or is my choice the main event, like choosing teams on the playground, with Jesus jumping up and down, shouting, "Pick me! Pick me!"? How can two choices coexist without one dominating or determining the other? Richard Foster's comment that "only the arrogant and the dogmatic find paradox hard to accept"[1] is appropriate, for we find dogmatic

Calvinists on one side facing off against equally dogmatic Arminians on the other.

God's Choice

I still remember a vivid conversation I had more than thirty years ago with a man I'll call Tom. His religious training taught him that if he happened to die while he doubted God or engaged in sin, he would go to hell. I shared with him some perspectives on the sovereignty of God, especially my tradition's belief that if we become God's child, God will never disown us. Tom replied, "But if you're saved once and for all, why go to church?" To Tom, worship and other religious activities were paying an obligation to stay right with God.

My friend Tom was right about one thing. We do owe a debt to God. If God is the sovereign king of the universe, we are all rebels setting up rival kingdoms where we can be in charge. This is true not just for the worst of us but for *all* of us: "For all have sinned and fall short of the glory of God" (Rom. 3:23). Our rebellion against God is something we cannot fix on our own, which leads us to an inevitable conclusion: we need outside help. Some of us realize early on that we need this outside help; some of us discover our need for it only after monumental struggle and suffering; some of us go through an entire lifetime thinking we're just as good or better than the next guy, and never think we need it at all.

The biblical term for this outside help is *grace*. Grace is help that can come only from God; grace is help that we do not deserve and can do nothing to merit or earn. And (if you're of the Calvinist persuasion) grace is help that, because we are dead in our sin (Eph. 2:1), we do not want to ask for or that we assume we will never need. Nevertheless, when we ask for help from God, here's what happens: "It is by grace you have been saved, through faith—and *this is not from yourselves*, it is the gift of God—not by works, so that no one can boast" (Eph. 2:8–9, emphasis added). This classic verse posits that nothing regarding salvation is our own doing; it implies even having faith is the gift of God.

But what if our salvation depended on our faith? A little voice at the back of our minds (at least my mind) asks, "Was your faith strong enough? Was it totally sincere? Were there no mental reservations?" If faith becomes a yardstick by which we are saved, how does the Lord deal with blasé, haphazard faith compared with hardcore, committed faith? I can easily find people around me who seem far more committed and full of faith than I am. How will I ever know if my little faith is enough? There is great comfort in believing that even my faith is ultimately a gift of God's grace.

A captain looked out from his bridge into a dark, stormy night and saw a faint light on the horizon coming straight at him. He immediately sent a message: "Alter your course 10 degrees south." Promptly, the reply came back: "Alter *your* course 10 degrees north." The captain was not used to having his commands ignored. He sent a second message: "Alter your course 10 degrees south. I am an admiral." Back came the reply: "Alter *your* course 10 degrees north. I am a seaman third class." Incensed, the captain ordered a third message: "Alter your course 10 degrees south. I am an aircraft carrier!" Back came the reply: "Alter *your* course 10 degrees north. I am a lighthouse." This is a Calvinist story. Humans enamored of their power of choice to move God have a surprise in store: God is the lighthouse!

Our Choice

I lived for years never questioning that I was the captain of my own soul; "making a decision for Christ" was how I entered into a saving relationship with God. Much of what I heard and read portrayed this decision as the crucial turning point in my existence. Although I never would have verbalized it this way, I must admit that somewhere in the recesses of my brain I took some pride in *my* decision setting everything in motion, especially compared with people who had not yet made such a choice.

The focus on *my* decision, however, slowly evaporated the awe and wonder and mystery of God like a pool of water in the desert; what was left at the bottom was a calcified deposit of formulas and doctrines. Where was the mysteriously sovereign God of Abraham, Isaac, and Jacob, who seemed to be such an actor on the stage of human history? God had become formulaic for me, a divine machine dispensing salvation if we deposit adequate faith and press the right button (say the correct prayer). My inner pendulum began to swing away from this small-time, bureaucrat god, who only processed our choices, toward a much larger, more mysterious, sovereign God.

Gradually, my decision looked more and more like the tip of an iceberg. Below the waterline was what Augustine called the prevenient grace of God, grace that "came before" every decision I thought I was making by myself. Had God the Holy Spirit been working all along, strengthening me, wooing me, nudging me? I became more and more in awe of God's gracious choice beneath the surface of my life. I began to realize I made my decision for Christ only because Christ had first made a decision for me—even, according to the Bible, before the foundation of the world (Jer. 1:5; Ps. 139:15–16). I began to wonder if I had ever made what turned out to be a good decision without the fingerprints of the Holy Spirit all over it.

All this might convince me there is no paradox here at all, no tension between these contrasting truths of divine sovereignty and human freedom. I am the captain of my ship, but God is the lighthouse. Except for one thing. I've also made a ton of bad decisions in my life, and still do! Where do *they* come from? If the Holy Spirit is always there guiding me (especially after I became a Christian and God's Spirit began to dwell within me; see John 16:13), I must have the ability to ignore the Spirit's leading, squash his guidance, and choose to go my own stupid way. The Bible makes a strong case for this; we can indeed quench the Spirit (1 Thess. 5:19) and are justifiably responsible for what we do (James 1:13–15). Furthermore, the Scriptures speak of Jesus coming into the world "to seek and to save the lost" (Luke 19:10) and of God's "not wanting anyone to perish" (2 Peter 3:9). It is difficult to reconcile this robust picture of God's desire for "all people to be saved" (1 Tim. 2:4) if humans have no choice and all is predetermined.

In his classic *Mere Christianity*, C. S. Lewis begins his defense of the Christian worldview by describing in detail the moral nature of human beings. Where does our inherent sense of right and wrong come from? Why do we feel guilty when we violate moral norms? Lewis sees this as evidence that God exists as the source of a moral universe and that we are created in God's image as moral beings ourselves. Adam and Eve seemed to have genuine freedom to choose to obey or disobey God in the garden of Eden; nothing in the text implies otherwise. Without allowing a free moral choice at this point, how could God hold all later humans responsible to face judgment and the penalty that Jesus Christ ultimately bears for them? Parents tell their children, "Actions have consequences." But such consequences are monstrously unfair if children have no choice in their actions. Moreover, anyone with pastoral experience knows that people agonize over their wrong choices and often agonize even more over their efforts to make correct choices. How do we explain all this unless there is the possibility of real human choice?

Looking through the Paradox

So who chooses first? I like the old illustration of a door that has written above it, "Believe in the Lord Jesus, and you will be saved" (Acts 16:31). When we exercise our human freedom to walk through the door, we turn around and see written above the door on the inside, "And all who were appointed for eternal life believed" (Acts 13:48).

God's sovereign choice and human freedom do indeed present a paradox. Just as light exists as both energy and matter—simultaneously exhibiting properties of waves and particles—so God's choice for us and our choice for God exist as different facets of the same reality. Scientists joke about thinking of light as particles on Mondays, Wednesdays, and Fridays and as waves on Tuesdays, Thursdays, and Saturdays; perhaps we should do our thinking about God's election and human freedom in a similar fashion.

History shows just how difficult it has been for both sides of this paradox to vibrate freely in tension with one another; yet only then do we hear the sweet note that rises from all the biblical evidence. After an exhaustive study of biblical literature, D. A. Carson concludes that this tension is indeed inescapable, "except by moving so far from the biblical data that either the picture of God or the picture of man bears little resemblance to their portraits as assembled from the scriptural texts themselves."[2] It is a crucial point. This paradox in particular is one where taking *some* biblical evidence to its logical conclusion violates *other* biblical evidence. Taking predestination to its logical conclusion, for example, seems to violate all we know about God's love and justice. Taking human free will to its logical conclusion seems to violate the sovereignty of God.

How might we listen for the pure note produced by both tines of this paradox, rather than lose it by emphasizing one tine over the other? Carson returns to the transcendent and personal nature of God, reflecting that "the way transcendence and personality combine is obscure to finite personal beings. . . . [Yet] the combination of the transcendent and personal in one being, God, lies at the heart of the sovereignty/responsibility tension."[3]

As personal beings, we have some idea about what choosing means. God is a personal being who also chooses, yet God transcends our space/time existence, so we really have no idea what choosing means for God. Our Creator's choices are not commensurate with the choices we creatures make; they aren't even in the same ballpark. God's way of choosing *is itself* a mystery to us! However, as soon as we speak about who chooses first (divine sovereignty versus human freedom, God's intentions versus our intentions), we begin to treat God like any other creature.[4]

We remember again the difference between duck decoys and real ducks; God is ontologically different from us. This might lead us to conclude that God's choices and our choices do not *necessarily* exclude each other: "For we understand neither what divine agency is (since God is transcendent) nor what creaturely freedom is (since human beings, as the image of God, are *like* God, neither sheerly determined nor sheerly undetermined), and so we have no grounds whatsoever for assuming that one of them must exclude the other. Instead, acknowledging mystery at this point gives us a deeper, richer picture of both."[5]

Thus, in the matter of salvation, it is possible to imagine that God's choice for me and my choice for God might mysteriously coexist.

As we look through this paradox, one arena of Christian life illuminated is God's will and my will: the issue of guidance. Do I choose first—make my own plans and life decisions and then (perhaps as an afterthought) ask God to bless them? Or does God choose first—create a detailed plan for my life that I must discover and implement step by step in order to be happy and fulfilled? Are God's will and my will mutually exclusive, or might they coexist? Through this paradox, we might conclude that just as divine sovereignty can underlie human freedom without negating it, so God's will can underlie my will. For example, if I totally surrender my will to God's will and want nothing but God's plans for my life, what happens when I discover God's plans for me? I must reengage my will! As some of us have experienced only too well, it often takes a *stronger* will to act on God's marching orders. Thus we live paradoxically: throwing down our will at God's feet, only to take it up again as soon as God calls us to do something. Without engaging our will, how can we do anything?

In my story about driving through the fog, I shared how genuine mystery shows us what we know (or can see) by clarifying it against the far larger background of what we do not know (or cannot see). I will see more of God's will as I move forward; landmarks hazy now will become clearer as I progress. I can earnestly follow the will of God I do see, without becoming immobilized by anxiety because I do not see everything. If divine guidance is truly another mystery, then the things I know can be seen only against the larger background of how much I do not know; stopping the car and refusing to move until all the fog disappears is not an option.

Finally, just as we have seen that it is an error to assume that God's choices and my choices are commensurate, so it may be with God's will and my will: might I be in line with God's will even when my will is bent in the opposite direction from what I assume God desires? Some of us look back on our lives and have those stories to tell.

Reflection Questions

1. If you tend to land on the "human responsibility/free will" side of this paradox, do an experiment and see how many times God's choice or predestination shows up in these passages: Matthew 22:14; Jeremiah 1:5; Mark 4:10–12; Ephesians 1:3–5; Romans 8:28–30; 1 Corinthians 2:7; Acts 4:27–28; Psalm 139:16; Romans 9:15–18; Exodus 4:21; Romans 9:22–24 (these verses speak of objects of God's wrath that are destined for destruction); Ephesians 2:8–10; Acts 13:48.

2. If you tend to land on the "divine sovereignty/election" side of this paradox, do an experiment and see how many times human choice shows up in these passages: Deuteronomy 30:19; Joshua 24:15; Ezekiel 18:32; Mark 16:16; Romans 10:9; Matthew 9:29; 1 Thessalonians 4:14; John 3:16; 2 Corinthians 5:15; Jeremiah 18:7–10; 1 Timothy 2:3–4; 2 Peter 3:9.

3. What does it mean to you, as you reflect on your own spiritual journey, that your salvation is both God's election and your choice?

4. How is the discussion of "finding God's will" helpful to you?

Chapter 13

ALREADY... NOT YET

The opposite of a correct statement is a false statement. But the opposite of a profound truth may be another profound truth.

—Niels Bohr

Like many, I grew up in a church culture that paid little attention to the kingdom of God. Eventually I came to realize that it is everywhere in the four gospels, mentioned 122 times, including 99 times from Jesus' own lips. Here in the earliest gospel, Mark, is our first glimpse of Jesus: "After John was put in prison, Jesus went into Galilee, proclaiming the *good news* of God. 'The time has come,' he said. 'The kingdom of God has come near. Repent and believe the *good news!*'" (Mark 1:14–15, emphasis added). The phrase "good news" brackets what Jesus announces as the good news, or the gospel. What he announces is *not* gaining forgiveness, eternal life, salvation, or heaven. The good news Jesus is bringing to the world is the kingdom of God.

Jesus says, "The time has come. The kingdom of God has come near." The Jewish people had been expecting the kingdom of God for a very long time, just as the Old Testament prophets predicted. One famous prophecy was Isaiah 61:1–2, which are the words Jesus chooses as the text for his sermon to the hometown crowd in Nazareth (Luke 4:16–30). His conclusion: "Today this scripture is fulfilled in your hearing" (v. 21). In other words, "Don't you see all of Isaiah's signs of the coming kingdom of God in my work?"

All creation started out very good (Gen. 1:31). But God's good creation came under the brutal tyranny of Satan. Now Jesus is leading a counterattack, recapturing the territory Satan has held. Whenever Jesus heals someone, the kingdom of God has come. Whenever he casts out a demon, the kingdom of God has come. Whenever Jesus reaches out to love people no one else loves—like lepers or tax collectors or prostitutes or sinners—the kingdom of God has come. Whenever truth and justice defeat injustice, the kingdom of God has come. Person by person, piece by piece, Jesus is reclaiming the territory that has been under the dominion of Satan. This is exactly what Revelation 11:15 looks forward to at the end of history: "The kingdom of the world has become the kingdom of our Lord and of his Messiah, and he will reign for ever and ever."

The Mystery of the Kingdom

The reframing nature of Jesus' parables, which we noted earlier, presses home the paradoxical, unexpected nature of the kingdom of God. The kingdom will not arrive in overpowering might, as the Jews expected, but is already at work quietly, as insignificant to human eyes as a mustard seed or a bit of leaven (Matt. 13:31–35). A tiny seed (750 mustard seeds to the gram), a tiny pinch of yeast. Jesus' kingdom looks embarrassingly small and weak against powerful world systems that seem to have the upper hand in every quarter. Yet he tells us it will expand to penetrate every corner of God's creation. As nineteenth-century Dutch theologian Abraham Kuyper famously maintained, "There is not a square inch in the whole domain of our human existence over which Christ, who is Sovereign over all, does not cry, Mine!"[1] Jesus is sovereign over all by right and is reclaiming human existence one square inch at a time, until the day when he will return and cry, "Mine!" in fact.

Other parables continue the beat of the kingdom's mystery. God's kingdom will not be joyously received everywhere, as the Jews expected; as we learn in the parable of the sower, it will never take root in some lives, it will be superficially received in others, and it will be choked out in still others (Matt. 13:1–9). One of the hardest truths for Jesus' audience, and many of us today, to swallow is how many people ultimately reject the kingdom (Matt. 7:13–14). Also contrary to Jewish expectation, the kingdom will not vanquish evil all at once but comingles with an evil world, like wheat and weeds growing together until the final judgment (Matt. 13:24–30, 36–43).

All these revealing yet hidden aspects of Jesus' parables of the kingdom have been well documented by New Testament scholars, premier among them George Ladd: "The new truth, now given to men by revelation in the person and mission of Jesus, is that the kingdom that is to come finally in apocalyptic power, as foreseen in Daniel, has in fact entered into the world in advance in a hidden form to work secretly within and among men."[2] Hence the classic phrase describing the kingdom of God: "already/not yet." Already here, but not yet reaching its fullness until Jesus returns. Pauline commentator Gordon Fee confirms that this "already/not yet" mystery of the kingdom is a controlling theme in Paul's letters as well. The future has already invaded the present, but not yet completely: "Death is ours (1 Cor. 3:22), but some still die (1 Cor. 11:30); the present and future are ours (1 Cor. 3:22), but the paradigm of present ethical life is our crucified Messiah (1 Cor. 4:10–13). Thus, Christian life is paradox, apparent contradictions held together in tension."[3]

Overcoming Dualism

As we explore the tension in the "already/not yet" kingdom of God, we observe that this particular paradox has been especially susceptible to dualities—to split apart what God wants to hold together. Jesus claims every square inch of creation for his kingdom, yet we often assign only certain compartments of life to the kingdom and label the rest of life "worldly" and outside the kingdom.

One such dualism is the kingdom of God encompassing a limited, sacred sphere of life; everything else is secular. Sacred music, art, and literature honor God; everything else does not. Sacred work (pastoring, evangelism, and so on) is valuable to God; secular work is not. In a colorful expression I never heard before living in Ethiopia, work in any profession or career except full-time ministry is "making bricks for Pharaoh"; a person works (makes bricks) in order to live, but only serving in church ministries counts as working for God (and only if the person serves full-time).

Another dualism is the well-known dichotomy between evangelism and social ministries, with churches commonly emphasizing one side while neglecting the other. As many of us who have been around churches awhile know, it is not uncommon for people who prioritize evangelism to accuse people interested in social action of "not doing kingdom work," and (of course) vice versa.

A similar dualism separates the present from the future. Some envision the kingdom of God being established only in the future (think of many African American spirituals); others insist that the kingdom can be experienced in its fullness here and now. (This optimistic view receded after the horrors of two world wars and lost further momentum as the twentieth century continued.) Closely akin to this "future/present" dualism is a "human/divine" dualism. Some assume the kingdom of God can be implemented if we humans just work hard enough; others assume the kingdom of God is solely God's work, with no human partnership allowed or needed. Such dualistic views of hope usually lead to either an unfaithful activism (we trust our own efforts far too much) or an equally unfaithful quietism (we disengage and wait for heaven).

Yet another prominent dualism throughout church history has been the dualism of law and grace. Some Christian communities focus on law, which can result in viral forms of judgmental legalism with little grace or forgiveness. Others proclaim themselves people of grace, which can lead to fluid ethical and moral values and minimal expectations. Theologians find law and grace constantly interpenetrating and correcting one another throughout the Bible. Certainly this tension of law and grace is present in Jesus' vision for his kingdom.

Echoing Abraham Kuyper, Eugene Peterson challenges all of these dualisms: "The Kingdom of God that Jesus announces as present here and now is not a religious piece of the world pie that God takes a special interest in and enlists us, his followers, to partake of and be filled with, a world that specializes in prayer and worship, giving witness and doing good deeds. No, it comprises Everything and Everyone."[4] When the two sides of the kingdom of God are not held together, it loses its power to impact the world as God intends.

A Supercollider

The dualisms we've surveyed are familiar points of debate in coffee shops or church board meetings. In *The Promise of Paradox*, Parker Palmer believes dualistc thinking is tempting for all of us: "We are not well prepared to understand our lives in terms of paradox. Instead, we have been taught to see and think in dualities. . . . But the deeper truths of our lives seem to need paradox for full expression. There is truth in both [sides of a paradox], and we live most creatively when we live between them in tension."[5]

The more we embrace one side of the kingdom of God more than its opposite, the more we exit the zone of their creative tension. I imagine this creative zone as the force field generated by the immensely powerful electromagnets in supercolliders, their magnetic fields propelling atomic particles through a forty- or fifty-mile oval conduit. Repeated revolutions around the racetrack build incredible speed until the particles slam like a cue ball into a tiny fragment of subatomic material. From such collisions, physicists learn clues to the beginning of the universe. Just as the energy of the supercollider comes from opposite magnetic forces in finely tuned tension with one another, so I imagine God's supernatural kingdom-creating power. Eminent twentieth-century physicist Niels Bohr maintains, "The opposite of a correct statement is a false statement. But the opposite of a profound truth may be another profound truth."[6]

I was a guest preacher at a church in Addis Ababa, Ethiopia, chatting with the pastor before the service. He told how the area of town where he founded his church was once full of prostitutes, but now six years later you never saw any prostitutes around his church. In his worldview, the sacred and holy influence of his congregation had sent the secular and unholy prostitutes packing! Unfortunately, such thinking does not square with Jesus' own kingdom understanding of what he was all about, especially concerning prostitutes (Matt. 21:31–32).

Another Ethiopian pastor (a student of mine) served a church in the same red-light district. Instead of driving prostitutes away, this pastor developed a ministry to them, meeting basic needs like food, health care, and education but also confronting the human trafficking of young girls from the countryside who were often sold into this life by their families. As might be imagined, many of these girls who were loved so unconditionally became followers of Jesus Christ—a perfect demonstration of how living in the tension between social action and evangelism empowers Jesus' kingdom.

What might happen if we reject the false dualisms and choose instead to live within the "already/not yet" tensions of the kingdom of God? Indeed, how might our neighborhoods, communities, and world be transformed as energized kingdom of God people are propelled outward, colliding with poverty, despair, and human misery? That would be an experiment worth trying.

Reflection Questions

1. Before reading this chapter, what came to mind when you heard the term "kingdom of God"?

2. Which aspect of Jesus' teaching on the mystery of the kingdom is most surprising or prominent to you?

3. Of the several dualisms mentioned, which in your observation most inhibits the power of the kingdom of God to change the world?

4. Where have you personally seen the energy of the kingdom of God at work?

PART 4

THE TWO HANDLES

Chapter 14

THE TWO HANDLES

*We want not an amalgam or compromise, but both things
at the top of their energy . . . both burning.*
— G. K. Chesterton, *Orthodoxy*

I often watched my grandfather dig postholes on his farm with an old-fashioned auger. It was shaped like a giant corkscrew, and my grandfather needed both strength and balance to push on one handle while simultaneously pulling on the other. Under his practiced hands, every half turn caused the auger to bite a little deeper into the hard Nebraska soil.

Nothing is more useless than a one-handled auger! Even with two handles, early on I noticed that maximum effect was achieved only when both hands were positioned at the very ends of each handle. The closer the hands are together on the handles, the harder it becomes to turn the auger, until eventually it's impossible. For really difficult jobs, my grandfather had a device that extended both handles to exert even greater torque on the auger's shaft.

In part 2, we explored how Jesus used playful paradox to capture his audiences' attention, challenge their mental, emotional, or cultural worldviews, and reframe reality to lead to systemic change. This first order of paradox is like a tightly wound spring: once it's sprung so the listener begins thinking or acting in new ways, the tension disappears.

In part 3, we looked at a paradoxical tension that is never resolved. Our image for this second order of paradox is a tuning fork—a harmonious paradox in which the two sides of the tuning fork, or two contrasting ideas, must vibrate in unison. Muffle one or the other even a little, and the pure note of biblical truth is not heard.

Now, in this section, we turn to yet a third order of paradox. The tension in two-handled paradoxes requires keeping the two sides of the paradox—like our hands on opposite handles of the auger—as far apart as possible.

Our guide into this wild territory is G. K. Chesterton, one of the most discerning and provocative observers of Christian paradox. Chesterton argues that Christian orthodoxy must resist minimizing the stark polarity of opposite extremes: "It hates that evolution of black into white which is tantamount to a dirty gray. . . . All that I am urging here can be expressed by saying that Christianity sought in most of these cases to keep two colors coexistent but pure."[1] Chesterton's description is especially true of the paradoxes we will look at in this section. Unlike the two tines of the harmonious paradox that vibrate together to create a greater truth, the two handles of these third-order paradoxes must be kept as separate and distinct as possible. The worst thing to do is to whittle even a fraction off either end.

Listen to Chesterton, in his classic *Orthodoxy*: "It was only a matter of an inch; but an inch is everything when you are balancing. The Church could not afford to swerve a hair's breadth on some things if she was to continue her great and daring experiment of the irregular equilibrium."[2] Once one idea becomes less powerful, another idea will inevitably become too powerful: "It was no flock of sheep the Christian shepherd was leading, but a herd of bulls and tigers, of terrible ideals and devouring doctrines, each one of them strong enough to turn to a false religion and lay waste the world."[3]

The past two thousand years of Christian history show just how critical it has been to keep these terrible ideals and devouring doctrines distinct and in check. When the early church was deciding how to imagine God as the Trinitarian three-in-one, even a single letter in a single word (*homoiousia* or *homoousia*) had momentous consequences. The debates about Jesus as being wholly God yet wholly human often came down to what may have appeared to be only a matter of an inch.

An inch is indeed everything. If Jesus is just an inch more divine than human, or a millimeter more human than divine, a false religion is born that might lay waste the world. This order of paradox seems to especially express the *mystery of being*: the nature of humankind, the nature of Scripture, the nature of God as three in one, the nature of Jesus Christ as God and human.

One Whirling Adventure

Before we explore these paradoxes, I invite you to linger a moment longer with Chesterton's flowing imagination: "This is the thrilling romance of Orthodoxy. . . . It was the equilibrium of a man behind madly rushing horses, seeming to stoop this way and to sway that. . . . To have fallen into any of those open traps of error and exaggeration which fashion after fashion and sect after sect set along the historic path of Christendom—that would indeed have been simple. . . . But to have avoided them all has been one whirling adventure; and in my vision the heavenly chariot flies thundering through the ages, the dull heresies sprawling and prostrate, the wild truth reeling but erect."[4]

Chesterton's words fire my imagination. Like many people, I have wondered about what seemed to me to be trivial arguments over obscure points of Christian doctrine. Yet were they trivial? There is nothing trifling or boring about the wild ride—stooping one way and then swaying another, reeling but erect—through the paradoxical tensions of Scripture. A whirling adventure indeed!

Reflection Questions

1. G. K. Chesterton argues that some biblical paradoxes must be kept coexistent but pure, so that the black and white of opposing ideas do not coalesce into a dirty gray. What examples come to mind where this may be true?

2. How do you respond to Chesterton's "whirling adventure" metaphor for Christian faith? Have you ever felt this adventure as forcefully as he describes it?

3. Chesterton wrote of "the monstrous wars about small points of theology, the earthquakes of emotion about a gesture or a word." Did he overstate his case? Is it really this big a deal?

4. How does Chesterton's overall view of Christian reality fit with our theme of exploring the mystery of God?

Chapter 15

EAGLES AND HIPPOS

There is an eagle in me that wants to soar, and there is a
hippopotamus in me that wants to wallow in the mud.
—Carl Sandburg

Some of my students smiled uncomfortably, others were startled, a few maintained stoic indifference. I walked around my class of thirty Ethiopian master's degree students, placing a handful of dirt into each hand as I reiterated, "For dust you are and to dust you will return" (Gen. 3:19). We were discussing the nature of humanity, expressed in the Hebrew word *adamah* ("dust") from which comes the proper name Adam. Adam is a creature of dust (Gen. 2:7). As they pondered that they were made of the same gritty substance as the dirt in their hands, I asked them how they felt. "Low," "humble," and "I don't like to think this is what I am" were common answers. Many winced as I went on to cite that chimpanzees and humans share 96 percent of the same DNA.[1] My dusty demonstration was intended to expand their imagination of what it means to be human.

We Westerners more often attend to the earthy side of our existence ("I'm only human"), but my Ethiopian students had been raised in a culture that denies the material and focuses more on the heavenly.[2] To claim an identity as *dust* felt subliminally, if not consciously, repulsive to them.

Eagles and Hippos

We can name several tensions within our paradoxical humanity. First, we are creatures of dust, yet far more than material organisms. Blaise Pascal captures it in his epigram: "Man is only a reed, the weakest in nature, but he is a thinking reed."[3] The power of human intelligence has offered us technological mastery over our world never imagined by our ancestors. Yet our supercharged minds exist in bodies that are weak and fragile reeds. Infinitesimal viruses vanquish us. Chemical changes in our brains influence us far more than we may wish or often even realize.

With the animals, we share an existence influenced by hormones and instincts, yet unlike the animals, we can make conscious choices against our instincts, what theologians call "self-transcendence."[4] We are always in process, transcending our impulses, cultures, traditions, previous worldviews, and even (or especially) our pasts. It is impossible to imagine human life without this passion for growth and development, even though it can be tragically stunted, arrested, or denied. Creatures of dust we are, but being human also means our reach constantly exceeds our grasp.

Consciousness itself is another aspect of the human paradox. However adept computers become in mimicking human thought, their behavior can be explained in strictly physical terms. Might the same be true for us? As we discover and map more and more of our brain activity, will we conclude that our minds can be reduced to a complex machine, a biological computer? Or is human consciousness an indefinable extra that transcends physicality—something no computer will ever achieve, the "ghost in the machine"? A group of philosophers called "new mysterians" suggest that the more we enhance the power of computers, the more we realize the paradoxical anomaly of human consciousness, which is inexplicable in solely materialistic terms.[5]

The tension between freedom and necessity is a third aspect of the paradoxical human landscape. Eugene Peterson puts it well: "Freedom does not mean doing whatever pops into our heads, like flapping our arms and jumping off a bridge, expecting to soar lazily across the river. Freedom is, in fact, incomprehensible without necessity."[6] This dialectic of freedom within boundaries (what Peterson calls necessity) is at the heart of the human condition.

Humans have genuine freedom but not unconditional freedom. In fact, we truly experience our freedom only in relationship to boundaries, from the laws of gravity to the laws of society. Thus genuine human freedom is in constant tension with significant boundaries we cannot escape, nor wish to, for then our freedom would disappear as well. Advertising executives speak of the "paradox of choice,"[7] having noticed we often freeze up when presented with no boundaries and too many choices: "Give us too little freedom and we'll stand up to dictators in Cairo and fighter planes in Libya. Give us too much freedom (and too many channels), and we'll sit in front of the TV, mindlessly flipping through our options, watching nothing."[8]

Finally, humans grow as individuals within community, another paradox. Hermits and loners are the exceptions that prove the rule. Without community, we are less than what we might be, even at the most basic level: babies need cuddling by other humans for normal development. We remain, and always will be, "ourselves," yet we discover much of who we are only through our interactions with parents, siblings, friends, peers, neighbors, and, more broadly, our tribe. While action films exalt the loner hero who turns his back on society, he (usually it's a he) answers the call of community in its time of need. "No man is an island," as John Donne famously declared. Most of us live most of the time in this paradoxical tension as individuals within community, neither swallowed up in a hive-like collective nor asserting a naked individuality.

Carl Sandburg elegantly reminds us, "There is an eagle in me that wants to soar, and there is a hippopotamus in me that wants to wallow in the mud." To be human is to be intimately aware of both the wind in our faces as we soar and the mud underneath our fingernails as we wallow. We are paradoxical to the core: controlled by hormones and instincts yet making rational choices that transcend them, existing as material beings yet having a consciousness that materialism cannot explain, possessing freedom that is genuinely free only when contained by boundaries, and achieving individuality through the influence of communities.

A Monster beyond Understanding

Blaise Pascal, a mathematical genius (Pascal's triangle) who was also a Christian mystic and apologist, is a worthy guide into this two-handled human paradox. In his collection of spiritual musings, *Pensées*, Pascal explains his approach to revealing the paradox of humanity: "If he vaunts himself, I abase him. If he abases himself, I vaunt him, and gainsay him always until he understands that he is a monster beyond understanding."[9]

It is clear that Pascal is working with a two-handled paradox—two extremes that must be kept as far apart as possible. Pascal continually pushes and pulls the opposing handles. If his opponent vaunts himself by exulting in his human potential, Pascal abases him by pushing on the handle of human fallibility. If his opponent abases himself, Pascal vaunts him by pulling on the handle of human dignity. This push/pull motion, Pascal believes, is necessary to drill through the topsoil of easy platitudes. As he bores ever deeper, eventually his listener discovers the paradoxical nature of humanity: a monster beyond understanding. (Pascal intends "monster" not in the sense of something fearful but as something unusual or unnatural—that is, beyond comprehension.)

This is the tension of opposite extremes so masterfully described by G. K. Chesterton. On these big issues, Christian faith has always vehemently resisted any bleeding of one side into the other, the black and white of clear opposites coalescing into a dirty gray. Only the two colors kept coexistent but pure adequately convey the truth.

Swiss Christian psychologist Paul Tournier concludes that this dual human nature offers an "eternal mystery," and comments, "This is what explains how man may appear so self-contradictory, how the best and worst are inextricably mixed together in him."[10] While no one would mistake me for a literary critic, I am not the first to notice that timeless literature often embodies this human paradox. Poor literature offers one-dimensional characters, stereotypical heroes and villains with obvious motives of good or evil. Better literature offers multidimensional characters struggling with their own mixed motives in ambiguous situations. Classic literature explicates, as Tournier says, the best and worst inextricably mixed together—good and evil, compassion and vengeance, altruism and selfishness—revealing it all in such a way that not only do we identify with the characters and the situations they face, but through them we better recognize our own inextricably mixed motives.

We have already seen that one of the attributes of mystery is conscious ignorance: we increase our understanding that there are things *beyond* our understanding, thus becoming more conscious of our own ignorance. Pascal uses the two-handled paradox to usher us into this mystery of our own humanity, which is beyond our understanding. How might the stark black-and-white clarity of the two-handled paradox lead us with awe and silence into the presence of this mystery?

Never Too High or Too Low

Some of our contemporaries regard human life as meaningless; we are insignificant beings adrift on a tiny planet in a backwater galaxy of a vast universe. Biblical theology agrees: "When I consider your heavens, the work of your fingers, the moon and the stars, which you have set in place, what is mankind that you are mindful of them, human beings that you care for them?" (Ps. 8:3–4). "Dust you are and to dust you will return" (Gen. 3:19). "The life of mortals is like grass, they flourish like a flower of the field; the wind blows over it and it is gone, and its place remembers it no more" (Ps. 103:15–16).

But the Bible goes far beyond despairing existentialists and suggests that while human life is not meaningless, it is *evil* at its core. The human gene pool is irretrievably contaminated by original sin.

All human pretensions to righteousness are "filthy rags" (Isa. 64:6). Human beings are sinners capable of outwardly brutal atrocities and inwardly rampant selfishness. Human life can be not only meaningless but depraved.

The opposite intellectual current in some quarters views human beings as the fountainhead of all value and meaning (famously expressed by Ayn Rand).[11] The Bible again goes this view one better: "You have made them [humans] a little lower than the angels and crowned them with glory and honor. You made them rulers over the works of your hands; you put everything under their feet" (Ps. 8:5–6). Human beings have inestimable value and purpose because they are made in God's image; they are the pinnacle of God's marvelous creation (Gen. 1:26). Ever since God walked with Adam as one friend with another in the cool of the garden (Gen. 3:8), no religion has held such an exalted view of human potential.

Chesterton reminds us that to adequately describe humanity, we must contradict ourselves: "In so far as I am Man, I am the chief of creatures. In so far as I am *a* man, I am the chief of sinners."[12] So also C. S. Lewis in the *Chronicles of Narnia*, when Aslan addresses Peter, Edmund, Susan, and Lucy: "'You come of the Lord Adam and the Lady Eve,' said Aslan. 'And that is both honor enough to erect the head of the poorest beggar, and shame enough to bow the shoulders of the greatest emperor on earth.'"[13]

Contradictions abound. Humanity's incredible potential for evil is matched by an opposing potential for good. With the same human tongue, we bless God and curse people (James 3:9). Mother Teresa and Adolph Hitler inhabit the same skin.

If anything, this contradiction is heightened when we turn to God's own people. Venerable Old Testament commentator Gerhard von Rad remarks concerning Abraham, "The bearer of the promise himself [is] the greatest enemy of the promise; for [the promise's] greatest threat comes from him."[14] Abraham bears the promise that God will create from him a people as limitless as the sand on the seashore; yet Abraham is also the greatest enemy of that promise by trying to achieve through human machinations God's promised son and heir. If Abraham is the headliner for this kind of paradoxical push/pull in the Old Testament, surely Peter plays a similar role in the Gospels—both the rock and a stumbling block to Jesus' mission (Matt. 16:18, 23). As goes paradoxical Peter, declares commentator F. Dale Bruner, so over the centuries we see the church itself: "The church is *both* Christ's main instrument and his main impediment."[15]

Pascal, our guide into the human paradox, sums it up succinctly: "Men never do evil so completely and cheerfully as when they do it from religious conviction."[16] From the Pharisees' persecution of Jesus, to Saul's persecution of the earliest Christians, to centuries of wars pitting Protestants against Catholics, history offers abundant evidence.

———

How might keeping these high and low views of humanity separate and distinct help us? First, accepting that life is paradoxical is a means of grace. Trappist monk Thomas Merton writes, "It is in the paradox itself, the paradox which was and is still a source of insecurity, that I have come to find the greatest security."[17] He goes on to explain why his paradoxical humanity is a means of God's grace: "I have become convinced that the very contradictions in my life are in some ways signs of God's mercy to me; if only because someone so complicated and so prone to confusion and self-defeat could hardly survive for long without special mercy."[18]

Our goal has consistently been to look *through* the window of paradox to see what it reveals, especially about God. As Merton looks through his own paradoxical humanity, he sees a God who, far from being put off by it, uses paradox as a channel of grace and mercy. Might we miss this grace and mercy if we succumb to either/or thinking and embrace only one side of ourselves, either the dusty or the heavenly?

Second, either/or thinking is often the strategy of Christianity's modern critics. G. K. Chesterton notes, "One rationalist had hardly done calling Christianity a nightmare before another began calling it a fool's paradise. . . . The state of the Christian could not be at once so comfortable that he was a coward to cling to it, and so uncomfortable that he was a fool to stand it."[19] Despairing existentialists like Jean-Paul Sartre judge Christianity to be a nightmare, lacking all human dignity and freedom; confident humanists like Richard Dawkins judge Christianity to be a head-in-the-sand fool's paradise, lacking all intellectual rigor.

However, when the two sides of paradoxical humanity are kept crisp and sharp, as G. K. Chesterton advises, the Christian worldview is *at the same time* more despairingly negative and more confidently positive than any alternative the world offers. Humanity biblically understood is ultimately more balanced, more able to assimilate disparate viewpoints, and more comprehensive of reality than either despairing existentialism or confident humanism. As Pascal knew, herein abides Christianity's greatness.

Third, when we absorb both high and low views of humanity into our spiritual bloodstream, it makes redemption more meaningful. As a young child saying my prayers at night, I remember asking my mother, "Am I a Christian?" and she replied, "Yes, Rich, you're a good boy." I grew up in a church that did not talk much about sin or the low views of humanity. A Christian was anyone who tried to live a good life and follow the Golden Rule. This background did not prepare me for the evil I eventually saw in myself, especially during angry conflicts that grew to borderline hatred of my father. It was not until I heard some '70s Jesus Freaks preaching on my campus that I realized what incredible *good* news owning a low view of my sinful self could be; it opened me up to the forgiveness and new life Jesus offered me.

Since then, my experience as both pastor and teacher of theology has convinced me that keeping the highs and lows of humanity crisp and distinct makes for a more robust view of Christ's redemption. Consider figure 1, which plots high and low views of creation, sin, and redemption.

When we have a lower view of the glory of humanity, it is often accompanied by a much less drastic view of sin, which usually then leads to a lower view of redemption (dotted line). This creates a relatively flat

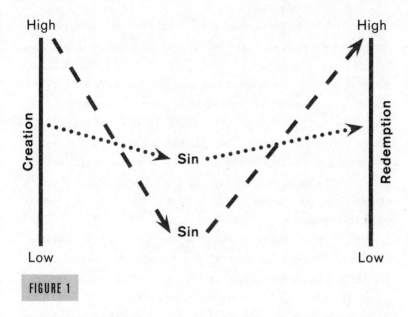

FIGURE 1

line from creation to redemption (and unfortunately brings to mind Jesus' words in Revelation 3:16: "Because you are lukewarm—neither hot nor cold—I am about to spit you out of my mouth").

However, when we have a high view of human beings as the pinnacle of creation with whom God walked in the garden, this tends to correspond with a precipitously lower view of sin as the loss of this intimate relationship with God, resulting in humanity's being warped away from God's good creation in every conceivable way. Such a lower view consequently requires a much higher view of redemption to achieve the return of humanity to its former lofty position (dashed line). The much steeper lines in this scenario better correspond with the biblical view of humanity, which is both extremely high and extremely low. Just as our celebration of Easter depends on how deeply we comprehend and experience Good Friday, so our gratitude for our redemption in Christ seems to track with how deeply we comprehend these highs and lows of our humanity. When I understood that being a Christian was far different from being a "good boy," I was ready to claim the redemption I had heard about occasionally in church but never thought I needed myself.

Finally, a fourth consequence of this "high/low" view of humanity is the ability to appreciate human culture without turning it into an idol. Some Christians focus so completely on the lows of human depravity that they are incapable of marveling at all that humanity has achieved. Yes, the church has always been corrupt, yet it has produced some of the most beautiful buildings, music, and art of the last thousand years. Yes, Isaiah is correct that "all our righteous acts are like filthy rags; we all shrivel up like a leaf, and like the wind our sins sweep us away" (Isa. 64:6). But in a well-intentioned effort to keep humanity in its place, we can miss the glory present in art, literature, music, science—indeed, any human endeavor.

Human achievements—whether by Christians or non-Christians— ultimately give glory *back* to the God who created us with the capacity for this creative self-transcendence. We create because we are made in the image of our Creator. When we understand our "high/low" para-doxical nature, we Christians, of all people, can most genuinely revel in the cultural achievements of our fellows yet still worship the God who planted the creative impulse within us.

Speaking of the human paradox, C. S. Lewis writes, "Our own composite existence is not the sheer anomaly it might seem to be, but a faint image of the Divine Incarnation itself—the same theme in a very minor key."[20] If Lewis is right, a great mystery is indeed afoot: humanity is a faint echo of the greatest paradox of all.

Reflection Questions

1. In your experience of human nature, do your first thoughts naturally tend more toward the positive ("vaunts himself") or the negative ("abases himself")?

2. What experiences have you had encountering the soaring eagle and wallowing hippo in your nature? Is it positive or negative to find both within you?

3. Do you agree that the paradoxical Christian view of humanity is superior to viewpoints that stress only high or low views of human life?

4. "Lord, what are human beings that you care for them, mere mortals that you think of them? They are like a breath; their days are like a fleeting shadow" (Ps. 144:3–4). How does this verse express both the value and the weakness of human beings?

Chapter 16

TREASURE AND VESSEL

The Bible is the Word of God given in the words of people in history.

—George Ladd, *A Theology of the New Testament*

Not only does the Bible contain the paradoxes we have been discussing, but the Bible itself is a paradox. G. C. Berkouwer, among others, draws attention to this paradoxical nature in what has been termed the "incarnational" character of Scripture.[1] Just as God in Christ emptied himself and became human (Phil. 2:6–8), thus conditioned by the earthly and the historical, so Scripture is God's own speech in human language. Just as we cannot strip a human veneer off Christ to reveal a divine inner substance, so we cannot strip away the humanity of Scripture. New Testament theologian George Ladd expressed it as "God's Word in human words." In describing this tension of the divine Word expressed through human words, Berkouwer writes, "This proclamation is a treasure in earthen vessels [2 Cor. 4:7], and the treasure does not fade and disappear in the fragility of the human instrument."[2] There is a difference between divine revelation and human language. Human language cannot hold all that reality contains. Any good poet or novelist knows this. Some aspects of reality are beyond any language's ability to describe or communicate. Biblical language, even when divinely inspired, is still human language. It is the human vessel that carries the treasure of God's revelation to us. Without the vessel, there would be no treasure. Yet any vessel can hold only so much.

Seeing Two Things at Once

This "treasure/vessel" paradox of Scripture reminds me of the faces/
vase drawing of Danish psychologist Edgar Rubin (fig. 2).

FIGURE 2

The Rubin drawing demonstrates figure-ground perception: our
brains perceive either a white figure (vase) on a black background
or a black figure (two human profiles facing each other) on a white
background. Our perception can flick back and forth between the
two images, but we cannot see both at the same time. I find that this
psychological quirk is also present in Scripture. If the divine authorship
of Scripture is emphasized, the human side becomes the background;
if the humanity of Scripture is in focus, its divine nature becomes the

background. In like manner, I find that focusing on the divine and human sides of Scripture simultaneously is hard (perhaps impossible) to achieve; we flick back and forth, yet must keep both distinct and clear in our minds, our hands at the very ends of both handles.

Frederick Schleiermacher, the nineteenth-century father of modern liberalism, believed that human reason must judge Scripture, separating the wheat of eternal concepts like the fatherhood of God or brotherhood of man from all the chaff the modern mindset could no longer accept, such as a virgin birth, Satan, or miracles. In Fred Craddock's piquant observation, "'Modern man,' whoever he was, seemed to be the measure of all things; he took his chair first, then the biblical furniture was arranged accordingly."[3] Schleiermacher collapsed the paradox by giving reason free rein to discard anything it found objectionable as it ferreted out the divine nuggets in what was essentially a human book created through various literary and historical processes; thus the handle of divine authorship and authority was slowly whittled away.

The early twentieth-century fundamentalist movement reacted against this flood sweeping away divine authority by filling intellectual sandbags that ultimately (as with liberalism) also depended on human reason. They proposed that God planted cognitive statements directly into the minds of biblical authors. The Bible thus becomes a set of propositions (like a lawyer's library of legal precepts) that reason can manipulate to set forth systematic truth.[4] As several have pointed out, what resulted does not square with the Bible we actually have.[5] Scripture is not an abstract set of principles but a diverse, multifaceted body of literature including history, hymns, poetry, proverbs, parables, and, most of all, *stories* that show God in action with real people in real historical and cultural situations. In their defense of the divine handle, they whittled away the human handle of Scripture.

We are left with two inadequate views. Liberals saw Scripture telling us little or nothing about God that was not conditioned by flawed and outdated human worldviews that modern reason could now confidently sweep aside; fundamentalists saw Scripture telling us a great deal about God through propositions dropped into authors' minds like emails in an in-box that the authors then simply copied and pasted into

Scripture. Neither view adequately embraces the tension of Scripture's paradoxical nature as God's Word in human words.

Exploring the Paradox of Scripture

In his classic *I and Thou*, Martin Buber offers a way of thinking about the early-twentieth-century debate between a liberal movement focusing on Scripture as human language and a conservative movement focusing on Scripture as divinely inspired propositional truth. Buber speaks of two kinds of relationships: I-It and I-Thou.[6] I-It is how we relate to an object; I-Thou is how we relate to another person. If the conservative movement was in danger of turning God into an It that could be mounted on a slide and studied through the microscope of the Bible, the liberal movement was in danger of turning God into a Thou who can be known only through personal encounter. Neither option does justice to Scripture: it is more than a collection of truths about God (I-It propositions), yet it is also more than the conduit by which we might experience God (I-Thou encounters).

Philosopher Arthur Holmes makes a valuable contribution by pointing out a middle way between I-It and I-Thou. He calls it *personal* language, described as I-She (or I-He, I-They).[7] Whether the person is another human being or God, personal language has certain characteristics.[8]

First, it is the product of *social existence*. It does not issue from an isolated intellect in a relational vacuum. Personal knowledge grows in community with others. Just so, God revealed his nature to Israel through historical events and preeminently in Jesus Christ through the historical community gathered around him; it is through the experienced witness of this human community (not as isolated intellects) that we come to know God ourselves.

Second, personal knowledge results from *shared bodily experience in a common world*. We can know other humans only through our points of contact as similar creatures. Likewise, we know God because God has created points of contact with us in our bodily existence, most fully in Jesus Christ, "God in the flesh." Thus we do not escape our material world to know God, as Greek mystery proposed. Our points of contact are "this-worldly."

Third, personal knowledge and language involve *emotions as well as intellect.* Neither our knowledge of other persons nor our knowledge of God is a matter of detached thinking alone. Both fluctuate between emotion and intellect.

Through his careful analysis of personal language as a third way between I-It and I-Thou, Holmes offers a way of preserving the truth and authority of Scripture without encasing it in a propositional strait-jacket. This is because "personal language is not confined to statements about objects, but conveys knowledge of other persons by stories and symbols and paradoxes and engaging dialog, by imperatives and exclamations, rhetorical questions and pleas. Scripture . . . is a richly diversified literature, not confined to objective descriptions and empirical statements about God; it presents God in action."[9] Such stories of God in action help us on our journey of knowing God as a person, not an object: "This is as personal as the way I talk about my wife. The terms I use and the stories I tell do not 'depersonalize' her; they make her a real person to you, and you feel you have met her whether or not you have ever seen her face to face."[10]

We began with the observation that just as God's self-revelation in Jesus Christ is a divine/human paradox, so Scripture has its own par-adoxical nature as divine/human speech, a treasure in earthen vessels. Arthur Holmes reminds us that the Bible is a rich diversity of literary forms, including paradox, each in its own way increasing our personal knowledge of God. Personal knowledge is a means to comprehend the divine/human nature of Scripture that is neither purely objective knowledge (I-It) nor purely subjective personal experience (I-Thou). We need not choose between them; in fact, we cannot. Both are needed to come to grips with the Scriptures as a faithful medium of God's self-revelation to humankind.

"The Pure Gospel Has Fingerprints All Over It"

Since our purpose has been not to look *at* paradox but rather to look *through* it, what might we see as we look through this divine/human tension in Scripture?

We might see a God who really loves earthy materiality. Ever since the New Testament era, the church has contended with a Greek worldview that material existence, if not downright evil, is certainly inferior to spiritual existence. This soul-greater-than-body, spiritual-greater-than-material dichotomized worldview can skew our view of Scripture. For example, some of my Ethiopian graduate students believed that admitting any human dimension tainted the Bible and degraded its purity. As Islam has been part of the Ethiopian landscape since the sixth century, I had the idea of contrasting the Bible with the Koran (table 2).

The Koran	The Bible
Dictated word for word	"Inspired," "God-breathed"
Produced primarily by one person over 22–23 years	Produced by many diverse authors over 1,500 years
Given in one language and culture (Arabic)	Given in three languages and diverse cultures
Definitive text in only one language: Arabic[a]	All cultures encouraged to translate and read it in their own language
Text is mostly precepts, laws, and principles to be memorized	Text includes a wide variety of literature, but especially narratives and stories
Is the ultimate revelation of God	Is the trustworthy means by which God's ultimate revelation in Jesus Christ is presented to us

[a] The Koran is now translated into 125 languages, but these are considered interpretations that do not carry the same authority as the Arabic text. Source: Prof. Kurt Christensen, private correspondence.

TABLE 2

As they pondered this chart, some of my students realized that their never-before-questioned assumptions about the Bible were, in fact, far more Muslim than Christian! When put side by side, the Bible is far more willing to involve and trust human beings throughout the revelatory process. The Bible is literally "breathed" into the minds of humans (2 Tim. 3:16), who then compose what they received into human words. The Bible emerges from a diversity of languages, cultures, and historical situations, rather than one data dump. The Bible's original languages have been translated and contextualized around the world, even though this vastly increases the possibility for misunderstanding or error. The Bible contains a far wider variety of literature, especially narratives or stories that were passed down through the centuries and require meaningful interpretation of the original context so each new generation can grasp their meaning. Finally, God's ultimate revelation is not a book but a human being, Jesus Christ, authoritatively introduced to us in the Bible. In Fred Craddock's finely tuned phrase, "the pure Gospel has fingerprints all over it."[11] If we see human fingerprints all over Scripture, surely this is what God intended!

Captivated Intellect

Looking through this paradox of Scripture, we might also begin to ponder the nuanced role of human reason in Christian faith. We will return to this in part 5, but as we have already seen, both sides of the liberal/fundamentalist debate inappropriately trusted in human reason.

Theologian Karl Barth writes, "[Faith] does not close our eyes but opens them. It does not destroy our intellect and compel us to sacrifice it, but it sets it free just as in a definite sense it captivates it for itself."[12] Barth argues that "reasoning one's way" into faith is impossible, and cites John Calvin's doctrine of the internal witness of the Holy Spirit, *not* the intellect, as the testimony for the truth and authority of Scripture. Calvin wrote, "Scripture will ultimately suffice for a saving knowledge of God only when its certainty is founded upon the inward persuasion of the Holy Spirit."[13] For Calvin, human arguments for biblical authority, or human testimonies about the reliability of Scripture, have their place. "But those who wish to prove to unbelievers that Scripture is the Word of God are acting foolishly, for only by faith can this be known."[14]

On the other hand, Barth affirms that faith does not stifle the intellect but encourages it to probe, explore, and discover the terrain of faith in the manner of Anselm of Canterbury's famous phrase, "faith seeking understanding." It was against the Enlightenment's elevation of human reason above the divine revelation in Scripture that Barth objected so vehemently. Once redeemed by faith, however, our reason truly comes alive! We can, without fear, intellectually explore as deeply as possible the human languages, cultures, and historical situations of Scripture. Barth's approach is sorely needed today, when some park their minds at the church door every Sunday while others let their intellectual preferences determine which parts of Scripture will have authority for them and which will not.

My personal experience has been exactly what Barth describes. In Barth's fine phrase, my intellect is freed but also captivated. Even though I cannot get my mind around all the paradoxes I find in Scripture, or even the paradoxical divine/human nature of Scripture itself, I am free to explore Scripture from the perspective of faith; I find my mind captivated as I do so.

Not an Owner's Manual but Empowering the Journey

Yet another way the paradoxical nature of Scripture helps us is in coming to terms with what the Bible should be *doing* in our lives. Have not many of us observed how Christians we know (maybe ourselves included) have a high view of biblical authority (using terms like *infallible* or *inerrant*), yet evidence little authentic biblical lifestyle in their daily living, such as caring for the poor or practicing self-sacrificing love? Critics who accuse Christians of being hypocritical are correct when we vigorously defend a book that has not shaped our own behavior. Whatever our theological stripe (I suggest that conservatives and liberals each have their own blind spots), arguing about the Bible has not seemed to help us live more biblically.

New Testament scholar N. T. Wright calls this paradoxical mystery of God's Word in human words "one of the [mysterious] points where heaven and earth overlap and interlock."[15] And here is a key point: we see this mysterious overlap of heaven and earth not only in the divine/ human *nature* of Scripture but also in the *purpose* of the Bible itself. I have often heard the purpose of Scripture explained using the analogy of an automobile owner's manual. The Bible provides detailed operating instructions to keep our lives running in top form, just as the owner's manual does for our cars. To the contrary, Wright envisions the Scriptures more like the mechanic who fixes our car, or the directions someone offers to help us get where we're going. "And where you're going is *to make God's new creation happen in his world*, not simply to find your own way unscathed through the old creation."[16]

The Bible is not a divine answer book about how to live a good human life. Scripture is the ongoing story of what God is doing in the world and how we can get in on it—the kingdom-of-God story of a new creation of all that God first intended, which went tragically wrong but can still be saved and redeemed.[17] Just as God chose to work through human authors in revelation, God chooses to work through human partners in his new creation. At neither point did God need to do so; other options were available. However, God's desire to work through us in this amazing story of salvation and new creation indicates a particular purpose for the Bible: "All Scripture is God-breathed and is useful for teaching, rebuking, correcting and training in righteousness, so that the servant of God may be *thoroughly equipped* for every good work" (2 Tim. 3:16–17, emphasis added).

The purpose of Scripture is to equip us for the work of heaven that overlaps earth. N. T. Wright again: "The Bible is there to enable God's people to be equipped to do God's work in God's world, not to give them an excuse to sit back smugly, knowing they possess all God's truth."[18] The temptations to fight about the Bible or to sit back smugly and assume we possess all of God's truth will always be with us. Looking *through* the paradoxical divine/human tension of Scripture helps us bypass old arguments and get to new places.

Reflection Questions

1. Before you read this chapter, had you ever encountered this paradoxical nature of God's Word in human words before? How?

2. Thinking of the vase/faces drawing, which side of Scripture—divine or human—do you normally see first, with the other filling in the background? Why might this be so for you?

3. How has the paradoxical nature of Scripture clarified or confused the role of your reason in your faith journey?

4. How has this chapter challenged you or deepened your understanding of the purpose of the Bible?

ALL FOR A LETTER

*I cannot think of the one without being quickly encircled by
the splendor of the three; nor can I discern the three without
being immediately led back to the one.*
—Gregory of Nazianzus, *On Holy Baptism*

One of my Ethiopian theology students had invited me to speak to
some youth leaders at her church. She guided us through many dark
streets as I dodged potholes, driving up the side of the mountain on
which Addis Ababa is built. Finally, we arrived at the building squeezed
into a tight urban block and were escorted to a small back room, where
about seven young adults waited for us. After a time of prayer, they
manhandled a huge wooden pulpit through the doorway into the tiny
room. Obviously, pastors used pulpits. I demurred and instead sat on a
plastic chair at eye level with them as they formed a semicircle around
me. I began to talk about the Trinity, the topic my student told me
these youth group leaders had requested.

Since my conversational Amharic was woefully inadequate, my
student served as translator. Only a few minutes into my talk, I noticed
something odd. I would pause for her to translate after two or three
sentences, but she went on speaking for thirty seconds or more. She
spoke with great emotion and many hand gestures. Even with my limited Amharic, I soon realized she was not only translating my words but
also embellishing all I said, sometimes even making points I had not

even mentioned! Several times she turned and said to me in English, "Tell them about this," reminding me of something we had discussed in class. As I went on, some of the youth leaders who knew enough English were now smiling to themselves as she translated. It ended up actually *her* talk far more than mine.

My greatest surprise, however, was discovering as I drove her home that this was *not* her own church after all; she had visited a few weeks earlier to speak to these same youth leaders about the Trinity. Because she was a woman, however, they did not give her their attention. Suddenly I put it together: she invited me along so she could teach them—through me—everything she wanted to communicate the first time! After we said goodnight, I drove home through the dark city with a bemused satisfaction. As I later told my wife how my student was so excited about what she had learned about the Trinity that she "used" me to share it with these leaders, I realized it was probably the greatest compliment I would ever get.

The Dance

Few of us begin our Christian journey with my student's passion for the Trinity. For me, the triune God was similar to the dusty, ancient farm equipment in a shed on my grandfather's farm—I was impressed with their venerable age but wondered what they were *for*. So is the Trinity—that ancient, venerable doctrine—for some of us. We wonder (if we think about it at all) how the three-in-one being of God makes any practical difference in our lives; it seems more at home in a theological museum than in everyday life.[1]

I track my student's excitement in knowing God as Trinity to the day we talked about *perichoresis*, an ancient term uniting the Greek words *peri* ("around": perimeter) and *choresis* ("dance": choreography), hence to dance or flow together.[2] Much to my students' amusement (they had never seen a professor so undignified), I danced around the classroom holding an imaginary partner, swirling faster and faster until I was a little dizzy, all the while talking about dance partners moving so synchronized that it is difficult to pick out one from the other. The dancers become one in the dance, even as they retain their individual identities.

Love, I went on to explain, needs partners, for love, despite Hollywood's best efforts to convince us to the contrary, is not a feeling but a relational *act* requiring a lover and a beloved. When the Bible says, "God is love" (1 John 4:16), it implies that God's essence is a relationship of love.[3] For all eternity, God has existed as a relationship or, if you will, a dance, of self-giving, other-directed love—the Father, Son, and Spirit each deferring in humility to the others and constantly saying, "No, you lead!" Creating human beings in God's own image is God's invitation to join this dance with God and one another.[4] For my student and others in her class, comprehending the possibility of human love flowing from this eternal Trinitarian love was like fireworks lighting up the sky.

At another class session, we spoke of creation as the *overflow* of God's own other-centered inner life.[5] God could have spent all eternity enjoying a full and complete relationship of mutual, self-giving love; God lacked nothing. Yet God chose to create a universe, including other sentient beings, to share this life-in-relationship. Look at the amazing overflow: a universe with at least a billion times a billion stars, a planet with 250,000 varieties of plants and 750,000 species of insects. My wife maintains God could have been a little less overflowing in that last area! Yet some of her favorite experiences have been snorkeling in the teeming coral reefs off the coast of Thailand and in the Red Sea: the varieties of fish are so stunning in all their permutations of size and color that a battalion of artists locked in a room for a year couldn't duplicate them.

If creation around us is only the overflow, imagine how rich and multifaceted must be the Trinitarian relational creativity of God to generate it all! Glimpsing new insights of God through the Trinity, my student wanted everyone she knew to get just as excited about the triune God as she was.

A Good Mystery

The only reason we know anything at all about the God of heaven and earth is that this God revealed himself to human beings just like us. God became known as the God of Abraham, Isaac, and Jacob because these individuals experienced God's messages, blessings, and presence in their lives. The Old Testament is not philosophical explorations—as Plato and Aristotle speculated about the Prime Mover, for example— but a collection of stories of God revealing himself in human events. The greatest story of all is of the Israelites experiencing firsthand the miracle of God leading them out of slavery from Egypt and into their promised land. Ever after, when they referred to God in their Scriptures, God was not an object of philosophy but "the LORD, who brought us up out of Egypt" (Jer. 2:6).

Now fast-forward many centuries. A man walked the dusty roads and verdant hillsides of Galilee making outrageous claims such as, "I and the Father are one" (John 10:30). Jesus spoke with the authority of God; he claimed God's power and prerogative to forgive sins; he judged as God judges. Yet Jesus regularly prayed to the Father, spoke about the Father as someone other than himself, and, on the cross, told his Father, "Into your hands I commit my spirit" (Luke 23:46). The more emphatic the early church became that Jesus Christ was in fact God incarnate—God in the flesh—the more pressure grew to clarify Jesus' relationship to the Father.

The situation was made more complicated by the early Christians' experience of God in yet another manner. On the day of Pentecost, just as Jesus promised, the Spirit of God flowed into them in a truly miraculous way. From that day forward, Christians knew that God was not only out there but also *inside them*. "You, however, are not in the realm of the flesh but are in the realm of the Spirit, if indeed the Spirit of God lives in you. And if anyone does not have the Spirit of Christ, they do not belong to Christ" (Rom. 8:9). So the Spirit (different from both the Father and Jesus) was also involved in human beings' experience of God.

British theologian Alister McGrath sums it up: "The doctrine of the Trinity wasn't *invented*—it was *uncovered*. . . . [I]t is the inevitable result of wrestling with the richness and complexity of the Christian experience of God."[6]

Humans *experienced* a God who created the world, whose glory is still reflected in the wonder of nature; a God who saved humans from ultimate darkness and death, whose tender love can be seen in the human face of Jesus Christ; a God who is personally present and active in the lives of believers. Uncovering the Trinity is like explorers entering a new land and drawing a map for people who will follow them. The mountains, rivers, and valleys are already there; the map simply pictures them in relationship to each other.

We are wise to remember at this point Saint Augustine's comment in the fourth century: "If you can comprehend it, it is not God." Clearly, we stand before a mystery. And it is a good mystery. Theologian Leonardo Boff writes that the Trinity "provokes reverence, the only possible attitude to what is supreme and final in our lives. Instead of strangling reason, it invites expansion of the mind and heart. It is not a mystery that leaves us dumb and terrified, but one that leaves us happy, singing and giving thanks. Mystery is like a cliff; we may not be able to scale it, but we can stand at the foot of it, touch it, praise its beauty. So it is with the mystery of the Trinity."[7]

All for a Letter

Although the mystery of a three-in-one God was not invented but uncovered in human experience, mentally putting the Three and One together is a struggle, begun by our spiritual ancestors, that continues to this day. Arius, perhaps the most famous heretic of the early Christian centuries, emphasized that Father, Son, and Spirit were distinct in their three-ness, but not really one: the Son and Spirit were lesser beings to the Father. Modalism, popular at roughly the same time, suggested that God took different roles (or "modes") in the drama of salvation (much as one actor might play different characters in the same play by donning different masks)—an image that promoted the oneness of God at the expense of a distinct three-ness.

The church wrestled mightily with the paradoxical three-in-one from the fourth through the sixth centuries. Prompted by the Arian challenge, the first ecumenical council at Nicaea (325 CE) proposed belief "in one Lord Jesus Christ, the Son of God, begotten of the Father, only-begotten, that is, from the substance [*ousia*] of the Father; God from God, Light from Light, Very God from Very God, begotten not made, of one substance [*homoousios*] with the Father." Was the oneness between the Father and the Son to be described as *homoiousia*, "likeness or coequality of substance," or *homoousia*, "unity of substance"?[8]

Notice the difference a single letter makes in this debate! Yet it was upon just such a small distinction that the integrity of the divine paradox depended: were the Father and Son absolutely one (seen through the lens of *ousia,* or substance) yet at the same time also truly distinct? We remember how G. K. Chesterton speaks of "only a matter of an inch," keeping the black and white of such paradoxes distinct and pure. Even a single letter can spell the difference between orthodoxy and heresy! Diogenes Allen returns to a now-familiar theme, pointing to the Trinity as a prime example of mystery helping us understand what we cannot understand: "It is rather the being of God, full and complete in itself, which leads us to invoke mystery at specific junctures in our reflections. It is by means of the intellect that we understand where it is impossible for us fully to understand. Such mystery does not lead to unbelief or agnosticism. As Gregory of Nyssa said, it leads to awe and silence in the presence of the divine *ousia*."[9]

———

At the end of the day, it is important to remember that our paradoxical concept of the Trinity is not reality itself. It is a mental model of reality, similar to a Tinker Toy assembly of balls and sticks forming a model of a molecule; the reality to which it points is incredibly greater than the model itself. As we have insisted throughout our explorations, we wish to look not only *at* the paradoxes of Scripture but also *through* them. As we look through the paradox of the Holy Trinity, what might we see?

First, we might see a different image of love. I began with the story of my student who became fascinated that the triune God is the center and source of Love. Love has been tragically degraded in our society, dumbed down into emotions, good times, or sex. Timothy Keller suggests that if the ultimate reality is indeed a community of persons who know and love one another, then "if you favor money, power and accomplishment over human relationships, you will dash yourself on the rocks of reality. When Jesus said you must lose yourself in service to find yourself (Mark 8:35), he was recounting what the Father, Son and Holy Spirit have been doing throughout all eternity."[10] Cornelius Plantinga offers a similar connection: "According to God's intelligence, the way to thrive is to help others to thrive; the way to flourish is to cause others to flourish; the way to fulfill yourself is to spend yourself. Jesus himself tried to get this lesson across to his disciples by washing their feet, hoping to ignite a little of the Trinitarian life in them."[11]

When it comes to love, I find people are most interested in specifics: what is the loving thing to do in this or that situation? While it is true that love always exists in concrete actions, perhaps we are wise to step back occasionally and see the big picture: we love because we are living out the nature, indeed the very being, of the God who is Love and created us like himself (in his image). "We love because he first loved us" (1 John 4:19). Let that truth get into our bloodstream and captivate our imagination; the specifics will come.

A second implication of the Trinity is a deep connection with creation. Consider *Avatar* (2009), the highest-grossing film of all time, breaking the record previously held for twelve years by *Titanic*.[12] It is set on the distant planet Pandora, where the alien society interpenetrates the life force underpinning their reality; they connect with this life force to save the life of the movie's hero, who rejects his fellow humans who are pillaging this peaceful planet and joins the aliens' fight against them. In the greedy strip-mining of this innocent society, we see allusions to the exploitation of both the environment and indigenous peoples over the centuries. We also see hints of classic New Age spirituality, especially a desire to stand against exploitation and be in harmony with the forces that underlie all reality.

While exploiters throughout history have at times looked for justification in the Bible,[13] the biblical worldview actually sides with the aliens in *Avatar*: the center of reality is a nurturing, relational, personal God (a very different God from an impersonal life force). "In the act of creation, God already manifests the self-communicating, other-affirming, communion-forming love that defines God's eternal triune reality. . . . God is eternally disposed to create, to give and share life with others. The welcome to others that is rooted in the triune life of God spills over, so to speak, in the act of creation."[14] The triune life of a nurturing, communion-forming, loving God spilling over into creation is a good image. Every person who comes to see this triune God spilling over into creation will naturally and passionately care about sustaining creation; creation begins not in the book of Genesis but in the being of the triune God. To not care about creation is to go against the flow of the very being of God.

Yet a third way we might benefit from looking through the paradox of the Trinity is to ask the question: how do we get in tune with the universe? Many spiritual seekers are asking exactly this question today. Here again, Christians already sit atop the mother lode of Mystery. Dallas Willard makes this point memorably in words that are worth quoting in full:

> The advantage of believing in the reality of the Trinity is not that we get an A from God for giving "the right answer." Remember, to believe something is to act as if it is so. To believe that two plus two equals four is to behave accordingly when trying to find out how many dollars or apples are in the house. The advantage of believing it is not that we can pass tests in arithmetic; it is that we can deal much more successfully with reality. Just try dealing with it as if two plus two equaled six.
>
> Hence, the advantage of *believing* in the Trinity is that we then live as if the Trinity is real: as if the cosmos environing us actually is, beyond all else, a self-sufficing community of unspeakable magnificent personal beings of boundless love, knowledge, and power. And, thus believing, our lives naturally integrate themselves, through our actions, into the reality of such a universe, just as with

two plus two equals four. In faith we rest ourselves upon the reality of the Trinity in action—and it graciously meets us. For it is there. And our lives are then enmeshed in the true world of God.[15]

I like Willard's word "enmeshed." Too often, our spiritual disciplines become pragmatic means to get what we want by pushing the right buttons on the heavenly vending machine. What if our spiritual practices were ways to get in tune with what God is *already* doing, where the deepest reality of the universe is *already* moving? Perhaps our spiritual habits like worship, prayer, Scripture reading, fasting, solitude, and the rest are like a surfer catching a wave. The ocean is so vast, so powerful, it is ridiculous to think we can determine its direction, let alone control it or bend it to our will. Instead, we give ourselves to it; we ride its waves and let them take us where they will, all the while "enmeshed in the true world of God."

Reflection Questions

1. Have you noticed any negative consequences when individuals—or local congregations or even entire denominations or Christian traditions—neglect one or more members of the Trinity in favor of another?

2. How does the ancient *perichoresis* dance metaphor expand or deepen your understanding of the relationship within the Father, Son, and Spirit?

3. Which (if any) of these practical consequences of the Trinity—love, creation, being in tune with the universe—make an impact on you?

4. How does the concept of God as three in one invite you into the mystery of God?

Chapter 18

THE ABSURD

*It is true that in Jesus Christ the mystery of the ground
of the world burns out more brightly than anywhere
else. But on the other hand, it is precisely in this light
that for the first time and definitively we grasp the true
incomprehensibility of God.*

—Hans Urs von Balthasar, *Elucidation*

When Hans Urs von Balthasar reminds us that with God's self-revelation in Jesus Christ, "it is precisely in this light that for the first time and definitively we grasp the true incomprehensibility of God,"[1] we see again that mystery hides even as it reveals. The apostle Paul writes that in God becoming a human being, "the revelation of the mystery hidden for long ages past" (Rom. 16:25), human and divine mystery coalesce. Jesus Christ pushes back the horizons of human mystery so that they open onto the divine mystery.[2] In Jesus, we especially meet the nature of mystery, knowing how much we don't know.

Theologian Paul Jewett wryly observes, "The more intimate the disciples became with Jesus, the less they understood him."[3] The first disciples are not one up on us for having seen Jesus in the flesh. Nor do we have an advantage over them by our perspective of two thousand years of history. Every person in every age confronts the same pivotal question. It is not, "Who do you say I am?" From Jesus' disciples to us today, Christians are still grappling to compose a complete answer to this question. No, the pivotal question is, "Will you follow me?" Now we are ready for a trek into paradox and mystery with one of history's more adventurous guides.

Three Kinds of Persons

Søren Kierkegaard (1813–1855) elicits one of three responses: some people love him, some hate him, many do not understand him. Unfortunately, Francis Schaeffer criticized Kierkegaard as the first existentialist thinker who crossed Schaeffer's famous "line of despair." This was a rush to judgment. Existentialist themes certainly appear in Kierkegaard's work, but his goal is different. Philosopher Diogenes Allen writes that Kierkegaard "was concerned to understand how to become and be a Christian, whereas existentialism is concerned with what it is to be a human being."[4] In fact, Kierkegaard championed evangelical themes, such as a personal relationship with Christ and understanding faith as a life of passionate commitment.

Mid-nineteenth-century Danish Lutheranism had turned Christianity into cool, detached intellectualism. Becoming a Christian came to mean being born into the state (Lutheran) church. Such a Christendom mindset that identifies Christian faith with a particular society, or culture within a society, has been part of our history since Emperor Theodosius made Christianity the state religion of the Roman Empire in 380 CE. In Kierkegaard's day, belief was depersonalized. It asked only mental assent that required no personal (existential!) commitment. In his book *Either/Or*, Kierkegaard exposes this refusal to commit, disguised as skeptical sophistication.

He begins with the *aesthetic person*, who is well versed in music, the arts, and a wide palette of sensual pleasures. At root, however, he or she is a mere spectator. We do not rush onto the stage in the middle of a play and shout, "Don't drink that cup, it's poisoned!" We are spectators. So is the aesthetic person. Aesthetes, Kierkegaard says, are like flat stones skipping across the surface of a pond; they must keep moving into ever more exotic or unusual experiences. If they lose momentum, they sink into nothingness. Kierkegaard especially opposes those spectators whose disdain of "fanatics" was an excuse to avoid real choices. The aesthete is ready to discuss the latest theory but never acts.

Kierkegaard next identifies the *ethical person*, who believes that Jesus' purpose is to promote ethical ideals. By following a set of principles found in the Bible, the ethical person assumes, he or she can become all that God expects. But this person misses or ignores the radical nature of sin. There is an "infinite qualitative difference" (Kierkegaard's well-known term) between humans and a "wholly other" God. Human reason or ethical effort can never bridge the gap between creature and Creator, the unholy and the Holy.

One of Kierkegaard's many parables brings this truth uncomfortably close to home. He imagines a land populated by ducks. Every Sunday morning all the ducks get up, brush out their feathers, and waddle to church. The duck preacher stands behind the pulpit and opens the duck Bible to the place where it speaks of God's greatest gift to ducks—wings! The duck preacher's sermon is eloquent: "With wings, you ducks can fly! You can mount up like eagles and soar in the heavens. You can escape pens and fences. The euphoria of complete freedom is yours. Give thanks to God for so great a gift as wings!" All the ducks in the congregation nod agreement and shout, "Amen!" Then they all waddle home again.[5]

For the ethical person, Jesus is reduced to a purveyor of ethical ideals ("You have wings!") that never transform anyone. Kierkegaard decries this state of affairs: "They have simply done away with Christ, cast him out and taken possession of his teaching, almost regarding him at last as one does an anonymous author—the doctrine is the principal thing, the whole thing."[6]

To become *religious* (Kierkegaard's third stage), people must admit the inadequacy of their efforts to live a worthy life in God's sight. Kierkegaard brought Jesus Christ back to the center of Christian faith in such a way that people would forsake debate on this or that doctrine and give themselves unreservedly, with "fear and trembling," into Christ's hands.

"Something Queer Is Going On"

Anyone who has plowed through Kierkegaard's dense prose has wished he could have addressed his task more succinctly! However, the broad outlines are clear. He focused on the paradox of the incarnation. How could Jesus of Nazareth be fully God and yet fully man?

Kierkegaard distinguished between a provisional and an absolute paradox.[7] In a provisional paradox, reason is employed to finally reconcile the opposite sides of the paradox. (Using this distinction, we saw that many of Jesus' paradoxical sayings are provisional.) With an absolute paradox such as Jesus Christ, however, reason is stymied. Reason is not prohibited or useless, although Kierkegaard has been falsely charged as an irrationalist. No, reason simply reaches a point beyond which it cannot proceed. Hence Kierkegaard's dictum that "reasons can be given to explain why no reasons can be given."[8]

Why is reason stymied? Because the incarnation proposes that a God outside of history has stepped into history and revealed himself. If God's self-revelation were completely amenable to historical categories—with evidence that could be used by reason to prove or disprove, in the manner of scientific method—then obviously we would not be dealing with a supernatural God. God is absolutely *other*, the great Unknown (God exists beyond history). Yet God is not *absolutely* other, because God became a human being (God entered our history).

Kierkegaard finds this paradox to be characteristic of the whole biblical account. This is not because he is so enraptured with paradox that he sees it behind every burning bush, or because he thinks God's nature is self-contradictory, or because he believes God delights in playing paradoxical games with us. No, paradox arises because God cannot communicate all of who he is through the medium of history, just as I could not communicate everything about myself to my five-year-old daughter. Roger Hazelton neatly summarizes: "The best God can do, then—although this course is dictated by our limitations and not his—is to create within history a disturbance which calls attention to the fact that something queer is going on. However, because the evidence itself can be nothing other than historical—which is all that we are capable of perceiving—the matter is most paradoxical."[9]

Kierkegaard lifts up God's problem and the resultant incarnation through his parable of a king who loves a peasant maiden.[10] How is the king to win the maiden's love? The easiest course would be simply to arrive on her humble doorstep in his regal splendor and announce his love for her. But this will not do. She will be so overwhelmed and dazzled by his presence that she cannot relate to the man behind the regalia. The king might whisk her away from her squalid life and elevate her to his side. But he wisely realizes that she will never be able to overcome her self-perception as a lowly maiden, even if clothed in queenly garments. What is the king to do? Suddenly he has it! He will wear peasants' clothes and visit the maiden as a lowly traveler, poor and hungry. In Kierkegaard's often-used term for the incarnation, the king will arrive "incognito." Alan Richardson offers an evocative description of this mystery of the incognito, whereby the revelation in Jesus Christ can be missed altogether: "He who is the Word Incarnate, speaks our language so perfectly, that no trace of a foreign accent is discernible, and he can readily be mistaken for one of ourselves, a native."[11]

Arriving incognito changes nothing, of course; he is still the king. But now, if he wins the maiden's love (and this is by no means guaranteed), it will be genuine love. It will be on her terms, not his. In like manner, Christ descended from his heavenly throne and "made himself nothing by taking the very nature of a servant, being made in human likeness" (Phil. 2:7). He is easily mistaken for a native. Thus, when we look at Jesus Christ, two options are always open: we can understand him as God-in-the-flesh, or we can understand him as a native—a great moral or ethical teacher, perhaps, but just another human being.

The Absurd

Kierkegaard called the absolute paradox that is Jesus Christ "the Absurd." Speaking into a culture of easy-believism, Kierkegaard chose a title that keeps challenging us, like a sesame seed caught between tooth and gum. He is not saying that Jesus himself is absurd or that we must believe absurdities. Rather, we reach a point where Jesus Christ is Absurd to human *reason*. Kierkegaard explains how: "The function of the understanding is to recognize the Absurd as such—and then leave it up to each and every man whether or not he will believe it. . . . The Absurd, the Paradox, is constructed so that the reason is by no means able of itself to resolve it into nonsense and show that it is nonsense."[12] Honest human reason reaches a point regarding the paradox of Jesus where it knows it cannot reach a conclusion: "No, it is a sign, an enigma, a composite enigma, of which the reason must say, 'I cannot solve it, it is not for me to understand it,' but from this it does not follow that it is nonsense."[13]

As we saw in our introduction to mystery, a conundrum or blank wall is not mysterious. Reason is perfectly capable of telling us, "It's just a blank wall," or, "It's just nonsense." Mystery is encountered when reason can tell us *some* things, but not *every* thing. In fact, the more reason can argue the case on either side of a paradox, the deeper the mystery. The car headlights dispel the fog, but as we follow their radiance farther into the fog, they reveal even more fog than we first realized was there.

What, then, can we do when reason ultimately fails before the mystery of God? This has been Kierkegaard's destination all along, pushing us out of our cozy nest of reason onto a limb where we are confronted (existentially!) with the truth that Christianity involves a choice, a leap of faith. Contrary to Kierkegaard's detractors, his famous leap of faith is not a blind leap in the dark.[14] Reason has resolved that in Jesus Christ we are facing a paradox that cannot be solved by reason alone. But during the process, reflection has uncovered solid evidence for choosing Jesus as God-in-the-flesh (for example: Jesus' actions and character as they shine through the Scriptures; the reactions of others to him; and so on). While the incarnation cannot be proven with historical evidence (the way Napoleon's defeat at Waterloo might be proven), neither is faith in Jesus as God-in-the-flesh a blind leap. Kierkegaard's leap of faith is *beyond* reason, but it is not *against* reason.[15] Diogenes Allen summarizes Kierkegaard's contribution: "Each person must venture in faith, which from the standpoint of 'objective thinking' is acting without sufficient reason. But actually a person who has faith *has* reasons for acting. Kierkegaard describes what *motivates* or moves a person to . . . respond with faith to the Christian gospel."[16]

───────────

Kierkegaard shows us not all biblical paradoxes are reserved for ivory tower contemplation. Jesus Christ as God-in-the-flesh forces us to make a real-life choice, the greatest and most far-reaching decision of our lives. All other personal decisions—whom we marry, what career we pursue, where we live—pale in comparison. Kierkegaard forces us to face head-on the Absurd paradox of Jesus Christ as the undeniable core of Christian faith.

Someone might reply, "But I'm not an intellectual. I'd never be caught dead reading Kierkegaard! What good is all this talk about 'the Absurd' to me?"

For years, I led what I called seeker groups in my home, inviting people who wondered whether the Christian faith was viable for them. Every person sitting in my living room might have been either an *aesthetic* person (wondering whether this Jesus offered a novel spiritual experience or would cramp their lifestyle) or an *ethical* person (assuming they were doing an adequate job of living however they defined a "good life," and wondering why they needed anything else, especially a Savior).

All knew a little about Jesus, but to move their hands to the very ends of these opposing handles—a man 100 percent human just like them, yet also the God who created them—indeed often sounded absurd. In Roger Hazelton's fine phrase, quoted earlier, the incarnation is "a disturbance which calls attention to the fact that something queer is going on." If they hung around the group long enough, then pondering this disturbance eventually led them beyond the safely speculative, "Who do people say I am?" to the personal choice, "Come, follow me." Not all answered that call, but they better understood what was at stake.

Even after we become followers of Jesus, however, the paradoxical push and pull of his divine and human natures is part of our ordinary, even daily, experience. We sing songs praising Jesus as our intimate friend, then minutes later listen to a sermon describing him as the sovereign King of Kings. We cry out to Jesus for help as we take an exam, believing he understands all our human needs, and then marvel at his creative majesty as we walk home along tree-lined streets in a kaleidoscope of fall colors. We are one minute supremely comforted that Jesus, sharing our humanity, "has been tempted in every way, just as we are" (Heb. 4:15), and the next minute embarrassed as we remember that he sees into our deepest personal darkness and that nothing is hidden from him (John 3:19–21).

The great Dane's fight against the Christendom of his day has parallels with our own. Whether we speak of a cultural religion of the Left (politically correct social action) or the Right (American exceptionalism blessed by God), in C. Stephen Evans's words, "Christendom tones down the radical character of God's demands on a person's life."[17] Kierkegaard will not have it. It is exactly this god-of-my-tribe that Kierkegaard has in his crosshairs. Jesus remains the Absurd—absurd to the Left that he would hold people to high standards of personal morality (Matt. 5–7), and absurd to the Right that he encouraged people to pay taxes (Matt. 22:19–21). As American Christianity increasingly splinters into polarized enclaves, Jesus Christ, the Absurd, explodes all our efforts to make him into the spiritual mascot for our particular cause.

We encounter again Chesterton's fear that the black and white of orthodoxy will meld into a dirty gray. Jesus Christ is human enough to care about our causes, yet God enough to transcend them and stand in judgment of them. He is domestic but never domesticated. "Godhead and manhood came together in a mysterious and incomprehensible union without confusion or change."[18] All of the major heresies of Christian history have whittled away at either Jesus' humanity or his divinity, often with cultural or even political motives.

Finally, Kierkegaard reminds us that God is far larger than human reason. In Kierkegaard's day, Christendom was a comfortable cul-de-sac where people thought they had God all figured out. Tony Campolo calls out this danger for us with a directness some may find troubling:

> Middle-class religion is uncomfortable with Kierkegaard's method
> for truth. The middle class likes things under control. Its people

are rational and want a religion that makes life easier and happier. They buy religious books that reduce Christianity to a reasonable plan for successful living. They seek churches that promise a healthy, optimistic suffering.

His truth is discovered through despair. His form of Christianity is out of sync with the culture. Middle-class religion explains what a person is supposed to think, but it fails to make people into Christians. It invites a person to accept reasoned-out, propositional statements about God but leaves him/her unconverted. It deludes people into believing that they are Christians if they give intellectual assent to theological statements.[19]

If there is a creator God, and *if* this God arrived incognito, entering our earthly existence as a human being, and *if* this God paradoxically retained 100 percent of his divinity even as he became 100 percent human, *then* this is a God worthy of our serious exploration, even though confronting the Absurd paradox in Jesus Christ eventually requires us to make a choice.

Reflection Questions

1. Does Kierkegaard's description of three types of persons—the aesthetic, the ethical, and the religious—square with your observations of people around you? If you are a Christian, which best describes you before you became a Christian?

2. How do you react to Jesus Christ, "the Absurd"? What is your response to how this played out in the author's seeker groups?

3. Is the issue of Christendom a live issue for you (or your church, if you have one) as it was for Kierkegaard? In what ways do you see it so?

4. Is the final quotation from Tony Campolo an overstatement, or a prophetic description of the dangers of middle-class religion today?

PART 5

THE SHELL

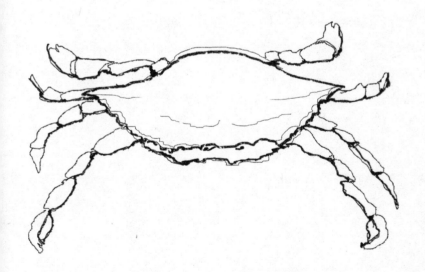

Chapter 19

THE SHELL

If the faith by which [the mind] lives does not allow it room to move, the mind is apt to exact its own revenge. A good mind denied by bad faith will self-destruct with insecurity, guilt, fanaticism, or doubt.

—Os Guinness, *Doubt*

I used to think birders were a little nerdy. Then I moved to Ethiopia. The variety of colors, sizes, shapes, and variety (twenty-three species endemic to Ethiopia alone) was mind-boggling for a Midwestern kid who grew up on sparrows, crows, and the occasional robin. Best of all, I didn't need to leave our porch: mouse birds fought each other for the rotting avocados that fell from our tree; masked weavers built nests hanging in the branches just above our porch; ibis regularly walked our lawn, pecking for grubs with their long beaks; black kites circled above us with their screeching cries and nested in the tall eucalyptus across the road; herons rose from the river beyond the trees; vultures held court on the rooftops across the way. I became a bird enthusiast, bettered only by my wife, who kept detailed notes about every new species she saw. She recorded it all in her bird book, which was filled with notations after four years. (One of our Ethiopian friends began calling it her "Bird Bible.")

At the same time that I was reveling in my new love of birds, I was teaching the theology of creation to Ethiopian graduate students. I was puzzled, then amazed, then alarmed, that most of my students saw no glory at all in creation. As I described the beauty of their country's birds, most responded with blank faces. What birds? If they were aware of birds at all, it was mostly as pests, rarely as objects of wonder. Many had grown up in impoverished situations; in their hierarchy of needs, reflecting on the glorious birds around them was rarely a priority. Similar experiences over my first two years in Africa started me on a journey investigating worldview, with the startling realization of just how pervasively our personal worldviews shape what we see.

As I struggled to communicate this worldview issue, one day in class the analogy of a shell popped into my mind. A crab's shell provides a safe and secure home. But as the crab grows, it must discard its old shell and create a new one. I described the empty crab shells we would find walking the beaches of California, their former occupants living dangerously until a new shell formed around them. In a several-week process called molting, crabs separate their bodies from their old shell even as they begin secreting a new, soft, paperlike shell beneath it to prepare for moving day. Without this natural process, the shell that was a protective haven eventually becomes a prison to the growing creature.

Our worldview is like the crab's shell. It provides a coherent perspective of reality, a mental "home" that is essential to our well-being. But as we mature and grow, we must discard our comfortable worldview for a larger one. Just like the crab, we repeat this process again and again as we move through life. Each transition can feel threatening as we discard our outdated picture of reality and create a new one. Oliver Wendell Holmes Sr. writes, "Every now and then a man's mind is stretched by a new idea or sensation, and *never shrinks back to its former dimensions*" (emphasis added).[1] Balancing the fear of change is the exhilaration of new ideas or insights.

Daniel Migliore describes the challenge of leaving behind our comfortable worldviews of God: "We fear questions that might lead us down roads we have not traveled before. We fear the disruption in our thinking, believing and living that might come from inquiring too deeply into God and God's purposes."[2] These fears are live issues for many of us, especially where the mystery of God is concerned. Better to let sleeping questions lie. But Migliore warns that fearing questions comes with a price: "As a result of these fears, we imprison our faith, allow it to become boring and stultifying, rather than releasing it to seek deeper understanding. When faith no longer frees people to ask hard questions, it becomes inhuman and dangerous. Unquestioning faith soon slips into ideology, superstition, fanaticism, self-indulgence and idolatry."[3] Most of us have observed this in others, if not in ourselves. "Faith seeks understanding passionately and relentlessly, or it languishes and eventually dies."[4] Like the crab's shell, our unquestioning worldviews can imprison and imperil our faith.

Renewing Imagination

Why did the worldviews of many of my students not register the glory of the birds that I saw so easily? I eventually concluded it was a failure of imagination. Make no mistake, my students had plenty of imagination. One Ethiopian denomination's strategic plan imagined reaching ten million new converts in just five years! Most US denominations would see this as insanity, not imagination! Why is our imagination so expansive in some areas and yet so constricted in others? I think it is worldview again. The material/spiritual divide in much of Ethiopian culture identified "spiritual" things as very important to God; issues like evangelism were thus lush areas where the imagination could roam and flourish. On the other hand, "material" things like birds were presumed to be of no account to God and therefore barren ground for imaginative interest.

In similar but often opposite ways, our Western worldviews warn our imagination that certain areas are not worth its time. Mystery is often one of these areas. Reason is our mother's milk in the Western world, and reason does not know what to do with mystery, especially the mystery of God. Moreover, our pragmatic age has no use for mystery, beyond perhaps providing a living for a few ivory tower academics. If we are going to take biblical paradox seriously, we need to expand our worldview. Often it is our imagination that first alerts us that our worldview is constricting our growth, turning what was once a home into a prison.

By speaking of imagination in these ways, I do not mean that there are not nonnegotiable truths in the historic creeds at the core of Christian faith. Imagination is not license to jettison orthodox boundaries and conjure up whatever we wish to believe. Rather, we can use our imagination to enter more fully into the *biblical* worldview. Is this not our goal: to have our worldview conform more and more to God's worldview? Can exploring paradox in Scripture renew our spiritual imagination to help us gain more of God's worldview? Such exploration itself requires imagination: "Only the imagination can . . . unify dissimilar elements and hold opposites in life-giving tension. Christians who are challenged to believe in this paradox . . . must be able to tolerate ambiguity and mystery."[5] Like the crab, can we move into a new worldview that welcomes paradox and delights in the mystery of God?

———

I repeatedly encounter imagination as I read through the corpus of Eugene Peterson, one of my favorite guides into the wild landscape of Scripture. In book after book, Peterson lifts up imagination as an essential ingredient of spiritual growth. Two sentences have especially stayed with me: "If we want to change our way of life, acquiring the right image is far more important than diligently exercising willpower. Willpower is a notoriously sputtery engine on which to rely for internal energy, but a right image silently and inexorably pulls us into its field of reality, which is also a field of energy."[6] Many of my valiant but futile New Year's resolutions show me just how sputtery an engine willpower can be!

Instead, we might explore images and imagination as a door into lasting change. Christians find these images in Scripture. Today, however, the imaginative world of Scripture that has shaped Western culture for centuries is fast disappearing, if it has not already vanished. In ages past, even unbelieving citizens knew the biblical story and were shaped by its worldview. Western civilization's literary imagination was soaked in biblical themes. Even the leaders of the Enlightenment, who sought an avowedly non-Christian Western culture, "were linguistically and imaginatively saturated with scripture."[7]

But according to George Lindbeck, the Bible is now "no longer a language with many senses, *a dwelling place of the imagination*."[8] What happens when this connection between Scripture and imagination is lost? Every group uses Scripture to advance its own agenda: "*Pietists* were wary of any use except that of legitimating and evoking a particular kind of religious experience; *legalists and social activists* looked only for directives for personal or collective behavior; the *rationalistically orthodox* used the Bible as a proof text for unchanging propositional doctrines; *fundamentalists* argued about its scientific accuracy and their opposite numbers, the *biblical critics*, treated Scripture as a set of clues for reconstructing what actually happened or was actually taught back in the days of Moses or Jesus" (emphasis added).[9] If Lindbeck is correct, Scripture is no longer engaged in the larger task of shaping imagination but is held captive to pragmatic ends; whether these ends are winning souls, liberating the oppressed, or defending or criticizing certain doctrines ultimately makes little difference.

Good Problems

In *An Experiment in Criticism*, C. S. Lewis argues that we read great literature because "[w]e want to see with other eyes, to imagine with other imaginations, to feel with other hearts, as well as our own. We demand windows. . . . One of the things we feel after reading a great work is 'I have got out.' Or from another point of view 'I have got in.'"[10]

Lewis goes on to distinguish two kinds of readers. One kind of reader *receives* from books; a second kind of reader *does things* with books. The first reader suspends judgment and allows the book to make its own impact. The second reader already has a use in mind. Lewis says of the second reader, "We are so busy doing things with the work that we give it too little chance to work on us. *Thus increasingly we meet only ourselves.*"[11] Whatever our theological stripe, we seem prone to create our own "fantasy Bible" like choosing the best players from across the league to create a fantasy football team. For our fantasy Bibles, we pick only those pieces that reflect the preferences of our preexisting worldview, and thus, we increasingly meet only ourselves.

Biblical scholar Abraham Heschel makes a similar observation to C. S. Lewis: "Hebrews learned in order to *revere*, the Greeks learned in order to *comprehend*, and modern people learn in order to *use*."[12] Is this not exactly the pragmatic temptation Lindbeck identifies—coming to Scripture not to revere or comprehend God but rather to use God for our own ends? Are we so busy doing things with Scripture that we have little opportunity to receive from it? What about "to see with other eyes, to imagine with other imaginations, to feel with other hearts"? If we never allow Scripture to challenge or change us—again in Lewis's poignant phrase—we increasingly meet only ourselves.

Rather than spoon-size bites, biblical paradox offers truths to gnaw on. We do not know what to do with it. It offers no immediate return. We find no use for it. It solves no problem. But what if we imagine a new kind of problem?

For the scientist, nothing is more important than choosing a good problem. The history of science can be read as the propitious choice of problems: good problems led to fruitful breakthroughs; poor problems (pursuit of the elusive philosopher's stone, for example) distracted capable minds for centuries and led to dead ends.

In Christian history, we see the same process at work. A proverbial problem for medieval scholastics was how many angels can dance on the head of a pin. Yet the early church fathers addressed good problems—God as three yet one, Jesus as divine yet human—resulting in monumental theological ideas we now often take for granted. What if they had chosen to invest those centuries of spiritual and intellectual energy in trivial problems?

Michael Polyani, a groundbreaking philosopher of science, writes that a good problem requires "an intimation of the coherence of hitherto not comprehended particulars . . . intimations of things hidden we may yet discover."[13] This sounds a great deal like the mystery we have been discussing—an intimation that there is more here than meets the eye, that there is deeper truth waiting to be discovered, that exploring this wild territory may be exciting (as well as frightening).

Cheryl's story, with which we began, presented a problem that was a "coherence of hitherto not comprehended particulars." In her problem, the juxtaposition of not-comprehended particulars involved human freedom and God's sovereignty. Friends she consulted did not define this as a good problem, probably either because it had no practical value or because it had no obvious solution. Yet Cheryl did not let it go. Pursuing this good problem opened up for her "a strange sort of comfort" both emotionally and intellectually: "I finally was able to rest in the fact that 'there is a God and I am not he.' . . . However, if I had not struggled, I never would have come to know that peace and comfort, as well as a deeper knowledge of God."

In today's bustling spiritual marketplace, we might think biblical paradox will rarely attract a crowd. And yet we experience in paradox a touch of the enigmatic, a hint of surprise and wonder, a street performer quality that captures our attention as we rush along the busy sidewalk so that we are compelled to stop and ask ourselves, How *does* he do that? In a pragmatic age, paradox can still arrest our attention—to present a good problem. Certainly this was true for Cheryl.

Redrawing Our Maps

Biblical paradox can offer us good problems. While we cannot *use* them, we can *receive* from them. What might we receive? We might "get out" into the larger landscape of God's awesome wonder and mystery; we might also "get in" on what God has been doing all along that we did not yet have eyes to see or ears to hear. There is little we can do with paradox. And yet (paradoxically!) there is much paradox can do for us. Paradox stimulates our imagination. As we imaginatively look through paradox, it helps us see what we may have missed before.

Our language is the means through which we see the world.[14] Eskimos have at least fifty words for snow; they "see" far more than I do.[15] This is not because their eyes are more astute but because they have far more words at their disposal to name and conceptualize what their eyes observe. When we neglect paradox, we miss developing a vocabulary that can enlarge our view of reality.

In *Freedom and Limit: A Dialogue between Literature and Christian*

Doctrine, Oxford theologian Paul Fiddes writes, "Unexpected imagery . . . seems to dissolve the world as we know it, to disintegrate the familiar in preparation for a new order."[16] He mines centuries of English literature for a rich understanding of the role of imagination in helping us see, including Samuel Taylor Coleridge's insight that imagination "dissolves, diffuses and dissipates, in order to create."[17]

I experienced Coleridge's dictum as a new and inexperienced Young Life leader. My supervisor told me I was beginning a continual process of freezing and unfreezing: how I understood high school kids would thaw and melt, then be refrozen in new forms, then thaw and melt again. Imagination aids in dissolving or thawing old worldviews even while creating new ones.

In another analogy, Scott Peck suggests growth is a lifelong process of "redrawing our maps," a process he hopes will continue until we die.[18] What entices (or prods!) us to keep exploring outside our comfortably mapped worldviews? Often it's our imagination! We see beyond our grasp and, by God's grace, venture beyond our understanding. My all-time favorite epigram about the power of imagination to stimulate change comes from Antoine de Saint-Exupéry: "If you want to build a ship, don't drum up the men to gather wood, divide the work, and give orders. Instead, teach them to yearn for the vast and endless sea."[19]

Up to now, we have explored individual paradoxes. Although frustrating, paradoxes can become good problems for us. Many unearth our yearning for something more—more understanding, more completeness, more holistic faith, more trust in God. In this last section, we will move from specific paradoxes to paradox as a whole. As our faith grows, the worldview that provides faith's home must grow and enlarge accordingly. If our worldviews do not transition and grow, they threaten to stifle and imprison our faith. Biblical paradox offers an essential ingredient in our spiritual growth—it stimulates our imagination, and imagination becomes a catalyst for enlarging our worldviews. We will look at four areas where this stimulation can lead to spiritual growth: faith, reason, hope, and finally, the mystery of God.

Reflection Questions

1. Do you agree that our faith, like the crab, needs to keep growing and expanding or else "it languishes and eventually dies"?

2. Have you ever considered that your imagination might be important in your spiritual life? What new thoughts has this chapter prompted?

3. How do you react to C. S. Lewis's discussion of two kinds of readers—those who "receive" versus those who "use"? Does this throw any light on your approach to the Bible?

4. Can you think of a good problem you have encountered? What happened?

Chapter 20

IF NOT CERTAINTY...

*Today I'm going to explain to you the unexplainable. I'm
going to define the indefinable. I'm going to ponder the
imponderable. I'm going to unscrew the inscrutable.*
— Deep South revival preacher

Early on, we observed that the equations created by Sir Isaac Newton are adequate for most uses but will not work at the subatomic level. Scientists solve this problem by speaking of a domain of validity: Newtonian physics works well within one level of reality (planets and baseballs), while quantum mechanics works better in another (atoms and quarks). We then asked, Could not the same be true in knowing God? While our daily spiritual journey and nightly prayers have one domain of validity that may have little need for biblical paradox, the complete picture offered by both Scripture and human experience requires it, just as physical reality requires both Newtonian physics and quantum mechanics.

I propose that the paradoxes we encounter in the wilder regions of life and Scripture need not stifle our faith. In fact, paradox can *stimulate* our faith, especially stimulate the spiritual imagination that helps our faith grow. But how does this happen? How does something as seemingly irrational as paradox renew, broaden, or deepen our faith? Os Guinness replies, "The rationality of faith is implacably opposed to absurdity but has no quarrel with mystery. . . . When a Christian comes to faith his understanding and his trust go hand in hand, but as he continues in faith his trust may sometimes be called to go on by itself without his understanding."[1] We begin with this paradoxical tension between trust and understanding.

Classical theologians held in tension the *fides qua* and *fides quae*, the "how" of faith (trust) and the "what" of faith (knowledge).[2] The Heidelberg Catechism (1563) answers the question, "What is true faith?" by speaking of knowledge and trust: "It is not only a certain knowledge by which I accept as true all that God has revealed to us in his Word, but also a wholehearted trust which the Holy Spirit creates in me through the gospel, that, not only to others, but to me also God has given the forgiveness of sins, everlasting righteousness and salvation, out of sheer grace solely for the sake of Christ's saving work."[3]

Faith is both *certain knowledge* (what) and *wholehearted trust* (how). Faith can never be solely trust (detached from biblical content) or only knowledge (detached from personal commitment). Faith is like a knowing, trusting friendship—not simply knowing facts about a friend on the one hand, or blindly trusting the friend on the other hand. In friendship, knowledge and trust meld. In fact, Saint Augustine was adamant that only people who have friends can understand the meaning of faith.[4]

Having a good friend means knowledge: "He is generous," "She has a good sense of humor." But friendship is more than knowledge, no matter how accurate. Friendship includes trust, which grows through experience, through seeing a friend respond consistently in various situations. Just so, faith matures as knowledge and trust reinforce each other. We will look at how biblical paradox might imaginatively stimulate each of these aspects of faith.

Faith as Knowledge

Human beings retain unfathomable depths that even lifelong friends will not penetrate. When we ignore our friends' mystery, we diminish them and take them for granted. Predictability breeds overconfidence.

We become sloppy in attending to their uniqueness. Perhaps they become simply cogs in our wheel, meeting our needs because this is what we *expect* of them. What was once mutual—giving and receiving—becomes utilitarian, need-focused, pragmatic.

Of course, our friends' freedom or uniqueness has not disappeared. Our knowledge of them does not control them. Eventually they will do something that startles or surprises us. At these moments, the friendship may become fresh and vital again, with new opportunities for growth. If our confident knowledge had turned our friend into an object to us, reexperiencing their mystery helps us see them again as a subject.

If this scenario sounds familiar, it is the story of God's people throughout the Old Testament. Again and again, they assumed they had Yahweh figured out: an object, a god in their pocket. Time after time, their sloppy overconfidence caused them to miss or ignore God's directions. In circumstances spanning two thousand years, Yahweh reasserted that he is a free, often inscrutable Subject: "As the heavens are higher than the earth, so are my ways higher than your ways and my thoughts than your thoughts" (Isa. 55:9). God's mystery prevents us from becoming overconfident in the "what" of faith.

A. W. Tozer again reminds us just how much is at stake: "*We tend through a secret law of the soul to move toward our mental image of God. . . .* That our idea of God correspond as nearly as possible to the true being of God is of immense importance to us" (emphasis added).[5] Assuming we have God figured out is death to maturing faith: "Our real idea of God may lie buried under the rubbish of conventional religious notions and may require an intelligent and vigorous search before it is finally unearthed and exposed for what it is."[6]

We often overestimate our knowledge. Pico Iyer, writing about how the failure to find the vanished Malaysia Airlines Flight 370 after more than a year of international search dramatized our limitations, argues that our accelerating accumulation of data lulls us into believing we know more than we actually do. "Whatever the field of our expertise, most of us realize that the more data we acquire, the less, very often, we know."[7] Gardiner G. Hubbard, the first president of the National

Geographic Society, expressed the same sentiment back in 1888: "The more we know, the greater we find is our ignorance."[8]

When we overconfidently assume we have God figured out, biblical paradox gets in our faces; it shines a light on how little of God we really know; it stimulates our conscious ignorance. Returning to A. W. Tozer's words, paradox prods us "beyond our conventional religious notions" to begin an "intelligent and vigorous search" for what we really think about God. What a gift to growing faith this can be! Knowing *what we do not know* can be as important to growing faith as knowing what we do know. And paradoxically, the questions that most baffle us can offer the greatest opportunities for faith to mature and grow.

Faith as Trust

I earlier described the seeker groups that met in my living room. They usually attracted people with varying degrees of skepticism or hostility toward the Christian faith. Often their questions gravitated toward paradox: How can a loving God allow evil in the world? Is Jesus Christ really both divine and human? If salvation is all about God saving me, how is it really my choice? How does this Trinity thing make sense? They suspected Mark Twain was on target when he said religion is "believing something you know ain't true."

I found that biblical paradox performed an invaluable service for honest skeptics. It forced them to *use* their reason rather than smugly assume Christianity is irrational and dismiss it without an honest hearing.[9] Honest seekers eventually realize that even human reason has its limits. If God is truly God, God far surpasses anything the human mind can comprehend.

For seekers, it is often honestly encountering paradox that first facilitates a turn toward trusting Jesus Christ. Theologian Reinhold Niebuhr observes that most people construct rational systems to give their lives an "anchor of meaning."[10] Yet even the brightest among us encounter paradoxical questions or life events that slice the cables to our most trusted rational systems. Life events come wrapped in mystery that does not easily yield its secrets. Even the paradoxical tensions of our humanity—the soaring eagle and wallowing hippo—are at times more than we can bear. We realize that no anchor of meaning forged in our minds will ultimately hold. We need something more. In the process, we discover that we can (indeed, we must) follow Jesus Christ without first having every question answered. In other words, we *trust*.

For believers, especially those with some other anchor of meaning than Jesus himself (perhaps their biblical or doctrinal knowledge, or their service to God or church), paradox performs an equally healthy function. It shakes and rattles our systems until we acknowledge that no system is adequate. In short, for both seekers and believers, paradox exercises our faith muscles—it gives us opportunities to learn to trust.

Martin Luther's classic example of faith is a ship in a harbor. Faith, says Luther, is more than standing safely on the wharf and believing the ship *can* safely cross the ocean; it means casting off and leaving the harbor behind! Christian faith will always be a mixture of knowledge *and* trust: objective knowledge (we believe the ship is seaworthy and can get us across the ocean safely) and subjective trust (we step on board).

If Not Certainty . . .

Listen to how Reinhold Niebuhr expresses my thesis that paradox points us toward mystery: "Its purpose is not to mystify but to clarify, yet in such a way that it is mystery which is made clear."[11] Niebuhr goes on to make a crucial point: "The very fact that it [paradox] is self-contradictory helps to emphasize the mystery of what it tries to say, for it tacitly affirms its own inadequacy to express it. By so doing it serves to throw us back upon faith itself and keeps us dissatisfied with any formulation which can be devised."[12] Consider the variety of biblical paradoxes we have surveyed. All have this in common: since they cannot be captured in any formulation we devise, *they serve to throw us back upon faith itself.*

What does this mean for our daily Christian experience? We often forget (or perhaps never realized) that the goal of Christian faith is never certainty, especially a certainty that leaves no room for doubt. Jesus would not offer any extravagantly "certain" proofs, like jumping from the pinnacle of the temple (Matt. 4:5–7). Many witnesses of Jesus' miracles did not end up certain at all; in fact, the crowds all deserted him. Scripture paints faith in terms of knowledge and trust, not certainty: "I know *whom* I have believed, and am convinced that he is able to guard what I have *entrusted to him* until that day" (2 Tim. 1:12, emphasis added). Eschewing certainty, Lesslie Newbigin declares, "There is no insurance against risk. We are invited to make a personal commitment to a personal Lord and to entrust our lives to his service. We are promised that as we so commit ourselves, we shall be led step-by-step into a fuller understanding of the truth."[13]

God does not expect certainty; God asks for *faith*. "Now faith is the assurance of things hoped for, the conviction of things not seen" (Heb. 11:1 NRSV). Assurance and conviction are quite different from certainty.

And yet I crave certainty. I have been taught to crave it by my upbringing, my education, my worldview. I might intellectually agree that faith is a blend of understanding and trust, but I never quite relinquish my quest for certainty. That my understanding will grow but never be complete, that my need to trust will never end, that my ultimate security will never be in *what* I know but rather *whom* I know—all these remain uncongenial to some of us.

Living in an African culture, I met people who had very little certainty (including where their next meal was coming from), but great trust in God's sufficiency to meet their needs. I admired my students who at times struggled with what they knew, but never wavered in whom they knew. I was someone who felt certain about much in my life, so it was bracing to be immersed in a Christian culture that was uncertain about so much in day-to-day existence, yet supremely assured of one thing: "I *know* whom I have believed, and *am convinced* that he is able."

Eugene Peterson points us back to spiritual imagination: "Our *imagination can be a catalyst for faith* that the Spirit uses to create something out of nothing, the assurance of things hoped for, the conviction of things not seen" (emphasis added).[14]

Biblical paradox is an imaginative catalyst for growing faith in several ways: it challenges what we know (or think we know) so that we engage in an intelligent search that deepens our knowledge; it exercises our faith muscles so that we trust more even (or especially) when we do not understand; it cuts the cables to our familiar but inadequate anchors of meaning so we are thrown back upon faith itself. In all these ways, paradox stimulates faith in a God we can trust, but never be certain about; if we could be certain, we would not need faith. We are led step-by-step into a fuller understanding of the truth. But we never arrive. A Mystery.

Reflection Questions

1. Is the classical definition of faith combining *fides qua* and *fides quae* (trust and understanding) helpful? Have you seen examples where your spiritual life (or that of others you know) has veered too far in one direction and neglected the other?

2. Considering faith as knowledge, has a paradoxical experience ever challenged what you thought you knew about God so that your understanding increased?

3. Considering faith as trust, has a paradoxical experience ever helped you trust God more than you did?

4. Is the author's argument that certainty is not the goal of Christian faith startling and scary or warm and welcoming to you? Why?

Chapter 21

THREE TENSIONS

One should not think slightingly of the paradoxical; for paradox is the source of the thinker's passion, and the thinker without a paradox is like a lover without feeling: a paltry mediocrity.

—Søren Kierkegaard

One of the classic paradoxical tensions in our Christian experience is between faith and reason. We have encountered it often in our explorations but now address it directly. Faith without reason or reason without faith is not difficult to navigate; how faith and reason relate to one another is complicated. In a Western worldview that implicitly assumes the superiority of reason, many of our questions circle around "How can my reason accept faith?" In Ethiopia the prevailing worldview assumes the priority of faith, so my graduate theology students' questions often came from the opposite perspective, "How can my faith accept reason?" Since Western books defending the integrity of Christian faith often have titles like *Reasonable Faith*,[1] I told my students the book I expected one of them to write for their culture would be titled *Faithful Reason*. Indeed, one might generalize that the anguishing "clash of civilizations" today stems, at least in part, from the inability of reason-based and faith-based societies to fruitfully engage with or even understand one another.

According to systems theory, when two persons experience tension with one another, one of them often pulls a third person into the relationship, thus creating a triangle between the three of them. Such triangling siphons off into the third person the tension the first two were experiencing with each other. What happens when paradox is invited as the third person into the sometimes tense relationship between faith and reason? It may end up catching some of the tension reason already has with faith, or that faith already feels about reason. We will look at three ways I have observed this happening as biblical paradox enters the faith/reason debate.

Does Paradox Imply That Reason Is Unnecessary?

I remember a friend who had no use for reason in her Christian experience. She grew up in a quite conservative Christian culture, which included nonstop litmus test arguments over arcane points of doctrine to determine who the "real" believers were. She walked away from active participation in this somewhat oppressive Christian community; some years later she personally met Christ, and Jesus became a real presence in her life. She became involved in a different church, although she remains suspicious of argument and heady discussions; she wants to keep her faith simple.

Philosopher Ronald Hepburn addresses my friend's misgivings about arguments and reason in *Christianity and Paradox*.[2] He begins by agreeing that "paradoxical and near paradoxical language is the *staple* of accounts of God's nature and is not confined to rhetorical extravaganzas."[3] He then asks an important question: "When is a contradiction not a *mere* contradiction, but a sublime Paradox, a Mystery?"[4] Can we determine when a paradox is simply a muddle, a logical contradiction, and when it is a mystery, "an excusably stammering attempt to describe . . . an object too great for comprehension, but none the less real for that"?[5]

When Hepburn sets about separating the sheep from the goats, he concludes that little if any paradoxical talk about God passes muster.[6] His only recourse is to forsake rational thought altogether! "We are not argued into belief by apologists," Hepburn concludes, "but *converted by the impact of Jesus upon us* into accepting his authority as absolute" (emphasis added).[7] I find it remarkable that this skeptical intellectual, who walks through the open door of paradox and accepts the challenge to relentlessly lay bare the "muddles" of Christian faith, ends up at an orthodox, even evangelical, position: "converted by the impact of Jesus into accepting his authority as absolute." Hepburn follows (in far more sophisticated fashion) the path traced by my seeker groups: honest investigation eventually recognizes that a person cannot be rationally argued into faith in God. The paradoxical nature of Jesus Christ eventually requires us to make a decision or leap of faith (so Kierkegaard) based on Jesus' person, character, and claims.

While Hepburn sees this decision of faith as nonrational (*without* reason), I would argue that it is superrational (*beyond* reason, in the same way that supernatural is beyond natural). This is an important distinction. Hepburn mistakenly assumes that because a person cannot be reasoned *into* belief, rational arguments *leading to* belief are unnecessary. But these are surely two different things. Reason is essential both before and after a faith commitment.

C. S. Lewis, one of the twentieth century's great proponents of a rational Christianity, is a good example. Lewis also realizes no one can be argued into belief: "Doubtless, by definition, God was Reason itself. But would he also be 'reasonable' . . . Not the slightest assurance on that score was offered me. Total surrender, the absolute leap in the dark, was demanded."[8] Yet in his autobiography *Surprised by Joy*, he narrates how essential his reason was in his faith journey; his reason cleared away the intellectual underbrush that obscured his path toward faith.

After he became a Christian, Lewis's prodigious output as a Christian intellectual fully employed his reason, belying the assumption that reason is less useful "once you have faith." By engaging his reason to explore his faith, Lewis produced enduring books addressing questions on miracles, prayer, and Satan, among many others—a superb example of what we will discover in just a moment as "faith seeking understanding."

Does Paradox Imply That Faith Is Irrational?

Here is a second tension: does paradox mean our reason must accept irrational contradictions that undermine faith? The early Latin father Tertullian robustly that asserted the illogical is a mark of truth: "Just because it is absurd, it is to be believed; . . . it is certain, because it is impossible."[9] Few people today matriculate into Tertullian's "the more illogical, the better" school of thought. Just the opposite: might fooling around with paradox grease a slippery slope into illogic and irrelevancy? I regularly have conversations around this second tension. To sidestep this fearful slide into irrationality, it is commonly held that paradoxes are only *apparent* contradictions. We saw apparent contradictions displayed in the playful paradoxes of Jesus—the tension dissolves after doing its work in us. Yet our travels since then reveal there are many paradoxes where the contradictory tensions do *not* dissolve; in fact, they grow more intense the deeper we delve into them.

We can clarify this issue by returning to mystery itself. While logical contradiction is certainly a characteristic of mystery, it is neither a *necessary* nor *sufficient* condition.[10] It is not a necessary condition because contradiction is not present in all mysteries. Mystery may simply be incomprehensible, like the Christian claim that God can be intimately involved in the lives of several billion people at the same time, or the scientific claim that the light we see tonight in a twinkling star left the star billions of years ago.

On the other hand, contradiction is not a sufficient condition of mystery. Not all contradictions can be labeled mystery, for we remember there are also what Ronald Hepburn calls "muddles," things that simply don't make sense. We must retain our right to discriminate between muddles and genuine mystery. If not, we are back to Tertullian's "it is certain, because it is impossible."

In *The Mystery of God: Theology for Knowing the Unknowable*, Steven Boyer and Christopher Hall describe Flatland, a two-dimensional world of length and width but no height. To residents of Flatland, a cylinder will be recognized as a circle because their two-dimensional minds can perceive only the cylinder's circular base. A three-dimensional person observing the cylinder might tell the Flatlanders that, viewed from the side, the cylinder looks like a rectangle. A figure that is simultaneously circle and rectangle is a logical contradiction in the Flatlanders' two-dimensional world. If they believe in the revelation that a third dimension (height) exists, then they have a mystery; however, the Flatlanders have no resources to judge whether a cylinder that is simultaneously a circle and a rectangle is a genuine mystery or simply a logical contradiction. They conclude, "To insist that a mystery may be incomprehensible but cannot be incoherent, or that it may be 'above reason' but cannot be 'against reason,' is to insist that an apparent contradiction must not *really* appear contradictory—which is, in fact, to beg the question and deny mystery altogether."[11] To leave mystery open as a genuine option, we Flatlanders must entertain the notion that reality is larger than our means of perception can register.

Gordon Graham avoids the contradiction cul-de-sac with a different definition of paradox: "Paradox is thus not to be understood as a logical form akin to contradiction, conjunction or disjunction but rather something, anything, which is *intellectually objectionable but nevertheless unavoidable*" (emphasis added).[12] Graham goes on to make an astute observation: "Logic cannot take us by the throat and force us to do anything. If we discover that there is after all something whereof we cannot speak, we are, in principle at least, free to pass over it in silence."[13]

This is a telling point. Christians for millennia have refused to pass over in silence the logical contradictions of the incarnation or Trinity, as well as many other biblical paradoxes. There is something more at stake, and more compelling, than mere logic. As Boyer and Hall conclude, "If we allow for mystery at all, then we should be prepared for real logical tensions."[14] Reason need not fear that paradox will lead faith into logical irrelevancy.

Does Paradox Imply That the Holy Spirit Is Irrelevant?

We have been investigating how biblical paradox enters the relationship between reason and faith. We first discussed that faith might use paradox as its justification that it has no need of reason and can get along fine without it, therefore concluding faith is *nonrational* (without reason). We then looked at how reason might see in paradox confirmation of its suspicion that faith itself is logically contradictory and flawed, therefore concluding faith is *irrational* (against reason). Now we briefly consider a third potential problem: faith using paradox to demonstrate just how clueless reason is about faith, since paradox seems to neglect the Holy Spirit.

Faith's accusation might sound like this: "All this talk of paradox sounds like dry-as-dust, overrationalized nonsense. Who needs all this intellectual fussing with paradox to encounter the mystery of God? Don't you realize that God is powerfully present in our personal experience every day through the Holy Spirit?"

I would reply that it is in our personal experience that we bump into paradox. We do not go seeking paradox; it finds us! Events simultaneously pull us in opposite directions and we are forced to live within the paradoxical tensions they create (e.g., try harder, eagle/hippo). Our personal experience with God immerses us in paradoxical tensions (e.g., God's choice/our choice, beyond us/with us, already/not yet). Throughout the Scriptures, it is human experience of God that shapes ideas of God—this human experience of God includes paradox (e.g., Three/One, divine/human, transcendent/immanent). Even the treasure/vessel nature of Scripture itself is paradoxical. These paradoxical tensions are not imposed on our personal experience; they originate within it.

After an especially powerful worship experience, someone might say, "God was unbelievably close to me. I felt an awesome power and majesty just sweep me up into heaven." That sounds like a paradox! God's immanence ("unbelievably close") and God's transcendence ("awesome power and majesty") were glimpsed in the same experience. As we unpack such common experiences, we find ourselves encountering paradox more than we might recognize.

Like a kid launching a kite, our intellect runs along the ground tugging a paradox behind it. Might we not imagine that what lifts the paradox high into the sky is the wind of the Spirit (John 3:8)? Scripture is clear that God's Spirit (not human reason) leads us into all truth

(John 16:13). If paradox stimulates our imagination by opening windows into the mystery of God, we can be confident it is ultimately the Spirit who lifts us into God's mystery.

"Faith Seeking Understanding"

We began this chapter by recognizing that faith and reason are often in tension. Let me summarize the two main observations so far.

First, the journey toward faith requires intellectual processes. Reason is necessary to acquire basic knowledge of the life, death, and resurrection of Jesus Christ, as well as how the Bible claims these events impact all creation. Thus, whether our journey toward faith is short or long, complicated or straightforward, none of us makes this trip without understanding basic ideas. For some of us, a major part of this journey toward faith is also addressing crucial questions about the meaning of suffering, other religions, or the church's woeful complicity in so much human suffering throughout history. Reason is essential in honestly investigating such questions.

Second, faith is never solely an intellectual decision. Søren Kierkegaard demonstrated that reason is stymied by the Absurd, the paradox of a God/man. Reason can never marshal 100 percent certainty *for faith* in Jesus; neither can reason (when we're honest) generate conclusive evidence *against faith* in Jesus. Faith requires the risk of personal choice, a "leap of faith" (Kierkegaard), or an "absolute leap in the dark" (C. S. Lewis).

In the eleventh century, Anselm of Canterbury offered a classic formulation of how faith and reason fit together: "For I do not seek to understand in order to believe, but I believe in order to understand. For this too I believe, that *unless I believe, I shall not understand*" (emphasis added).[15] We assume it should be the other way around: first we have all our questions neatly ticked off, then we consider believing. Anselm maintains it is just the opposite, however, for the same reasons given by Kierkegaard—reason helps us in our journey, often crucially, but the moment comes when we must risk trusting God with our lives. Once we take that trusting step of faith, we naturally want to understand more and more of this new relationship with God and all its implications for our lives, hence "faith seeking understanding."

To summarize: faith does not depend on reason, yet faith cannot do without reason. We must find ways to live within this paradoxical tension. Perhaps we see faith and reason as static and predictable, two figures frozen into position. "Faith seeking understanding" invites us to think of them as a dance! Often faith is the leading partner, with reason struggling to keep up as they swirl around the dance floor. Other times reason takes the lead, steering faith away from tripping over potted plants (logical fallacies) or blundering around the floor in blind exuberance (joining a cult). If faith and reason are Fred Astaire and Ginger Rogers, each placing a foot where the other's has just been as they swirl together, the nuances of the dance are beautiful to behold (even if, occasionally, toes *do* get stepped on). If our investigations into paradox help us imagine this complex choreography and thus expand our view of faith and reason, we will be better equipped to live faithfully and intelligently in God's world.

Reflection Questions

1. When you began this book, did exploring biblical paradox suggest any dangers to you?

2. Thinking of the people you regularly interact with, might they see the Christian faith as nonrational, irrational, or something else? Why?

3. By the end of this chapter, were the roles of faith and reason in Christian faith clarified or made more confusing for you? What was clarified? What is more confusing?

4. Does the "faith seeking understanding" relationship of faith and reason make sense to you? What thoughts are stimulated for you in imagining them dancing together?

Chapter 22

SIMPLICITY AND COMPLEXITY

I would not give a fig for the simplicity this side of complexity, but I would give my life for the simplicity on the other side of complexity.

—Oliver Wendell Holmes Jr.

The epigraph to this chapter has stimulated my imagination since my university days. In the Christian life, paradox exemplifies such complexity. Settling for easy answers, trite slogans, and simplistic formulas is often our default position. Even so, I have been arguing that exploring these paradoxical complexities offers rich rewards. These final chapters offer hints or suggestions of the simplicity we might discover on the other side of such complexity. In this chapter, I want to ask, How does pressing into this paradoxical complexity renew our hope?

Hope already has a whiff of the paradoxical about it. Hope combines something tangible and concrete with an uncertain pathway or timeline in arriving. (If we unequivocally knew how to get there or exactly when we would arrive, hope would be superfluous, as Chicago Cubs baseball fans know only too well!) As we saw earlier, biblical faith combines knowledge and trust; so does hope. To see how exploring the mystery of God through paradox might stimulate and deepen our Christian hope, a small detour is first required.

How Do We Know?

There are three basic approaches to how we know. One approach, often called *realism*, assumes that reality exists "out there" (not just in my mind) and I can know it by interacting with the world around me. For example, scientists discover truth about the world by gathering observable evidence and following the scientific method in analyzing it. For much of the modern era, science has been the premier method of producing what has been called "objective" truth. Ever since René Descartes kicked off the Enlightenment era by proclaiming, "I think, therefore I am," this view has had supreme confidence in human reason to get to the truth of anything.

But what if reason is not the impartial and reliable guide to truth the modern world has assumed? In the last third of the twentieth century, this supreme trust in reason came under great scrutiny by a second approach known as *postmodernism*. (It is named for what it wants to replace: Enlightenment-inspired modernism.)[1] Here truth has no reality beyond the mind that believes it. Language becomes a key issue, for language is the means by which we construct (a key postmodern term) our own realities.

In the late twentieth century, Michael Polyani, Hungarian physicist and philosopher of science, demonstrated that human subjectivity plays a critical role even in science. All of us, scientists included, are not simply reasoning brains (as Descartes imagined) but complex beings including emotion and intuition. Thomas Kuhn, in his seminal *The Structure of Scientific Revolutions*, showed that scientific breakthroughs often happen through subjective leaps of human intuition called paradigm shifts.[2] In other words, the scientist's own paradigm (or worldview) determines how he or she approaches the data. For example, a social scientist spent years recording observational data about Navajo Indian life before realizing he had imported alien (Caucasian) concepts into his data. To properly understand what he observed, he needed to look at the data through concepts intrinsic to Navajo culture.[3] In the history of science, examples abound of an accepted worldview trumping data pointing in other directions (for example, clinging to an earth-centered solar system when the data clearly indicated otherwise).

Objective and subjective, observation and theory, thus bleed together. Michael Polyani's important conclusion is that *knowledge does not exist independent of a knower.*[4] In other words, there is no vantage point of pure and neutral objectivity where a scientist (or anyone else) can stand to evaluate anything, whether a different culture, the shape of the universe, or the claims of the Bible. We all bring our subjective predispositions into the process of knowing.

If we agree with Polyani that human subjectivity conditions how we know, the postmodern critique of modernism's claim to pure, impartial reason is correct. The modernist assumption to know reality with 100 percent clarity is now often labeled *naive realism*: there is still genuine reality "out there" (hence *realism*), but because of human subjectivity it is *naive* to assume that I (or anyone) conceptualize reality exactly as it really exists.

If we place naive realism and postmodernism on opposite ends of the "how we know" spectrum, we can now mention a third approach midway between them. It is called *critical realism*. Veteran missiologist Paul Hiebert describes its essence: "It is a form of realism, for it assumes a real world exists independently from human perceptions or opinions of it. It is critical, for it examines the process by which humans acquire knowledge and finds that this knowledge does not have a literal one-to-one correspondence with reality."[5] In this third approach, one can still believe "absolute" truth is out there; however, no one can claim to know this truth "absolutely"—that is, in a one-to-one correspondence with reality.

In his excellent study *Worldview: The History of a Concept*, David K. Naugle offers a simple baseball analogy to help us better understand these three ways of knowing.[6] A baseball umpire practicing naive realism might say, "There's balls and strikes, and I call them *the way they are.*" In other words, every pitch really is either a ball or a strike, and this umpire can see that reality without error and with 100 percent clarity.

A postmodern umpire replies, "There's balls and strikes, and they *ain't nothing until I call them."* In other words, a pitch could be in the dirt, but if he wants to call it a strike, it's a strike! This umpire's personal perception of each pitch (what he calls it) determines its reality.

Last of all is the critical realist umpire, who proclaims, "There's balls and strikes, and I call them *as I see them.*" In other words, every pitch is in reality either a ball or a strike, but he cannot call each one with 100 percent accuracy; he does the best he can (calls them as he sees them) while maintaining humility regarding his limitations.

A Way into Complexity . . . and Hope

With apologies for this philosophical detour, these three views of how we know allow us to make some observations about paradox and Christian hope.

A naive realism position has little incentive to explore the complexity of paradox. Here one's understanding of Scripture is in one-to-one correspondence with the reality Scripture describes ("I call them the way they are"). With such 100 percent clarity, there's not much complexity to worry about (and also nothing much to hope for).

What about the opposite position? In postmodernism, we become the authors of our own truth; we can sand off all the rough edges of the paradoxical complexities of Scripture until they smoothly fit together however seems best to us ("They ain't nothing until I call them"). Here again, there seems to be less need for hope. I judge naive realism and postmodernism both to settle for the simplicity on this side of complexity.

Readers have by now guessed that I believe critical realism best handles the complexity of biblical paradox. Because it is realism, it assumes the absolute truth of God behind the complexity. But because it is critical ("I call them as I see them"), it acknowledges that we now see "through a glass, darkly" (1 Cor. 13:12 KJV). The critical realist makes an enduring pursuit of the simplicity on the other side of complexity, tempered with great humility about the torturous path he or she must travel through complexity to get there.

I have found that the crucible in which a "living hope" (1 Peter 1:3) is forged is often the tension between a "sure and certain" outcome and an uncertain pathway toward it. Think of the tuning-fork and two-handled paradoxes already discussed; such a living hope is created when neither side of the tension—outcome nor pathway—is muffled or diluted.

Let me risk an example of one of the most divisive issues of our time: the church's response to homosexuality. Much of the energy surrounding this issue seems to have coalesced around the opposite poles of total rejection and total acceptance. Negativity, even hatred, expressed by people coming from a total rejection position has been deeply harmful to homosexuals. Would the Jesus who welcomed tax collectors, prostitutes, and sinners into his intimate fellowship (Matt. 21:31–32) not welcome homosexuals into his fellowship today? I am sure he would. And if so, how can we in the church not offer the same care and human dignity to people Jesus would welcome? On the other hand, I cannot go the way of total acceptance, for I believe that Scripture does not support same-gender sexual relations. I am somewhere in the middle. From conversations with those promoting total acceptance or total rejection positions, however, it is clear they assume that no middle position can (or should) exist.

I definitely find myself on a journey into complexity, along the way pleasing few and finding even fewer allies. Can I look forward to any simplicity on the other side of this complexity? I see it only in Jesus himself, who compassionately welcomed the woman caught in adultery and defended her to her morally superior accusers, but then privately directed her to go and sin no more (John 8:3–11).

How winsome is the simplicity of Jesus' blend of compassion and conviction! Living within this tension is beyond me, like a balance beam I can walk on for only a step or two before falling off one side or the other. How do individuals, congregations, even denominations walk this fine line that came so effortlessly and naturally to Jesus? I have no idea. But seeing it in Jesus gives me hope. I am certain there is simplicity on the other side of this complexity; I am utterly uncertain how to get there. Perhaps Jesus' Spirit can create the simplicity of his compassionate conviction and his convicting compassion in a few human beings, and they will help the rest of us imagine a third way between what are for me two inadequate options. This is my hope.

What about other, less emotionally fraught issues where Christians might find hope in wrestling with complexity rather than choosing between polar opposites? One is certainly the tired debate of evangelism versus the promotion of social justice. We might also include supernatural healing versus modern medicine, spiritual counseling versus psychological counseling, allegiance to country versus allegiance to God, and so on. Once we open our imagination to the many tensions that exist within our normal Christian experience, every reader might easily generate his or her own list. I expect our lists might be longer than we anticipate.

———————

Parker Palmer, one of my backcountry guides into paradox, writes in his introduction to *The Promise of Paradox*, "Contradictions, paradox, the tension of opposites: these have always been the heart of my experience, and I think I am not alone. I am tugged one way and then the other. My beliefs and my actions often seem at odds. My strengths are sometimes cancelled by my weaknesses. My self, and the world around me, seem more a study in dissonance than harmony of the integrated whole."[7]

We might not all claim Palmer's words for ourselves, although they certainly sound familiar to me. But I am more interested in his next two sentences: "Perhaps contradictions are not impediments to the spiritual life but an integral part of it. Through them we may learn that the power for life comes from God, not from us."[8]

As we consciously journey into the paradoxical complexity of life with God, whence comes our hope? Perhaps it begins with conscious ignorance, the byproduct of any engagement with mystery. Before we took biblical paradox seriously, we could rest in the simplicity on this side of complexity, perhaps confident that our views had a one-to-one correspondence with reality. But as we step into complexities that paradox reveals (whether by choice or by life events), we, who once thought we saw God's plans and purposes with absolute clarity, now realize we do not.

It is this move from naive realism to critical realism that stimulates our hope. We need to hope more than we did before. There is a certain end (the simplicity on the other side), but an extremely uncertain pathway toward it. As Parker Palmer says of his own wrestling with paradox, we learn that the power for life comes from God, not from us. Our hope now can rest only in God.

Reflection Questions

1. What is your reaction to the quotation, "I would not give a fig for the simplicity this side of complexity, but I would give my life for the simplicity on the other side of complexity"?

2. Which position best represents you on the "how we know" spectrum—naive realism, critical realism, or postmodernism? What, if any, difference do you think this makes?

3. Do you agree with the author that the critical realist position is the best one from which to understand Christian hope? Why?

4. How do you react to Parker Palmer's contention that contradictions in life show us that the power for life comes from God and not from us?

Chapter 23

COASTAL WATERS

When you are presented with something that you think to be not just accidentally mysterious but necessarily mysterious, there is always the danger that you have fallen into an obscurantist muddle. . . . Far worse is the superficiality that conceives nothing to be unfathomable because it has fished only in coastal waters.

—R. F. Holland, *Against Empiricism*

As stated in the epigraph to this chapter, the existence of the unfathomable in our lives, and especially in God, often may be missed because we have fished only in coastal waters. If we are willing, biblical paradox leads us offshore into deeper waters of the necessarily mysterious. As we conclude exploring biblical paradox and how it invites us to rediscover the mystery of God, we begin by quickly reviewing how mystery was understood in the ancient world.

Experienced in the frenzied psychedelic rites of first-century mystery religions, *pagan mystery* manipulates the supernatural world for knowledge and/or control of human life and destiny; this is seen also in contemporary expressions such as astrology, channeling, and all forms of the occult. Describing a mingling of strange bedfellows, C. S. Lewis writes, "For magic and applied science alike the problem is how to subdue reality to the wishes of men."[1] This common goal of bringing reality under human control underlies the historic rivalry between magic and science. Car dealerships aiming for the same midrange market are more keenly competitive with each other than either is with the Mercedes dealer down the road. But philosopher Michael Foster offers some sage advice at this point: "It is important now to distinguish biblical mystery from the mystery of pagan supernaturalism; especially in order that the scientist (not only the professional scientist but the scientist in all of us) may confront the Christian doctrine as it is. Otherwise it may look to him like only another example of the pagan superstition, which is dead but will not lie down."[2] It is tempting for the scientist in all of us to lump all mystery together, rejecting Christian mystery as just another form of pagan supernaturalism.

We encounter *Greek mystery* as we step away from pagan supernaturalism and begin moving toward biblical mystery. Contradicting the pagan desire to manipulate reality for human welfare, the Greek goal was "wondering contemplation of the divine, in which mystery was not dispelled but more fully revealed."[3] The Greek philosophers' basic assumption was that eternal reality unfolds before human contemplation because human reason itself is our connection with eternity. Diogenes Allen explains that it's a case of like knowing like: "The handiwork of mind which we see displayed around us in the order of the visible universe is essentially like our own. Reason in us, reason evident in the visible universe, and reason as the ultimate basis of the invisible universe are essentially alike, so we have the capacity to know ultimate things."[4] Thus, while pagan magic and science were always rivals, Greek mystery and science both trust human reason as the ultimate pathway to reality. Indeed, for the Greeks, contemplating mystery became intellectual worship: "Contemplation was the union of the divine element in man with the divine element in the universe."[5]

Mystery in Scripture

Turning to Scripture, we find that encounters with Yahweh narrated in the Old Testament are regularly marked by holy awe and mystery: Moses at the burning bush (Ex. 3:2–6) or on Mount Sinai (Ex. 33:11, 18–23), Elijah on Mount Horeb (1 Kings 19:9–18), Isaiah in the temple

(Isa. 6:1–4). Yahweh is seen as the revealer of mystery, as when King Nebuchadnezzar says to the prophet Daniel, "Surely your God is the God of gods and the Lord of kings and a revealer of mysteries, for you were able to reveal this mystery" (Dan. 2:47).

In Aramaic, the word *mystery* describes the sovereign decision of a king made known only to his innermost council and kept secret from others until revealed in its execution.[6] This image of king and council appears in the scene with God and his angels in the beginning of the book of Job (Job 1:6ff.) and, even more clearly, in the scene in which Isaiah hears the call, "Whom shall I send? And who will go for us?" (Isa. 6:8). Human wisdom cannot penetrate God's secrets; they must be revealed. Mystery in the Bible can thus be defined as "the secret thoughts, plans, and dispensations of God which are hidden from the human reason, as well as from all other comprehension below the divine level, and hence must be revealed to those for whom they are intended."[7] Yet by graciously choosing to reveal this mystery, God elevates himself above all false gods.

In the New Testament, mystery is revealed in a concrete historical event—the person and work of Jesus Christ (John 1:14, 18). In his later letters, the apostle Paul assures his readers that they have "the full riches of complete understanding, in order that they may know the mystery of God, namely, Christ, in whom are hidden all the treasures of wisdom and knowledge" (Col. 2:2–3). Louis Bouyer admirably summarizes, "The mystery in the end is that of Christ himself, not only as supremely revealed on his Cross but also as including within him from all eternity the whole plan for our race and for the whole universe."[8] Pursuing God's mystery is not endless speculation on the divine being or essence, as in Greek philosophy. It is not secret formulas to control human destiny, as in pagan mystery religions. It is openly "disclosed" (Col. 1:26), "made known" (Eph. 1:9), "made plain" (Eph. 3:9), and a "revelation" (Rom. 16:25) in Jesus Christ.

The mystery of Christ has two sides. On the one hand, it is entirely beyond the grasp of human wisdom. The mysterious wisdom of God is (1) prepared before the world began (1 Cor. 2:7), (2) concealed through the ages until its time for revelation arrives (1 Cor. 2:7; Eph. 3:9; Col.

1:26; Rom. 16:25–26), and (3) hidden in God, the Creator of all things (Eph. 3:9), who himself makes it known to us (Eph. 1:9). What human mind could ever aspire to all this? On the other hand, this mystery is not esoteric, ethereal, or in any way otherworldly. It is played out in concrete historical events, foremost in the cross itself (1 Cor. 2:2) but also demonstrated concretely in the church (Eph. 5:32) and in the remarkable inclusion of the Gentiles as heirs with Israel in the promises of God (Eph. 3:4–6).[9]

While this mystery is now out in the open, demonstrated in historical events for all who receive its good news, its riches are not thereby exhausted. "The glorious riches of this mystery, which is Christ in you, the hope of glory" (Col. 1:27), are inexhaustible. The breathtaking grandeur of Christ's mystery is displayed in Ephesians 3, where Paul sums up many of the themes of the hidden/revealed nature of God's mystery discussed above: "Although I am less than the least of all the Lord's people, this grace was given me: to preach to the Gentiles the boundless riches of Christ, and to make plain to everyone the administration of this mystery, which for ages past was kept hidden in God, who created all things" (Eph. 3:8–9).

This passage is a wonderful corrective to the assumption that because Christ, the fountainhead of God's mystery, has been revealed, the Christian faith is now without mystery! To assume we know the width and length and height and depth of the mystery of God's love in Jesus Christ is to fish only in coastal waters. Paul's doxology at the close of this passage fittingly glorifies this mysterious Lord "who is able to do immeasurably more than all we ask or imagine" (Eph. 3:20).

A Rotary Telephone?

The mystery of God articulated by Paul excites the mind and emotions even as it stimulates the will; exploring this mystery is, perhaps, the greatest of all human adventures. Why is it not pursued more avidly today? Some Christians see the mystery of God as a black rotary-dial telephone in a cellular age: more suitable for a museum (theology class) or the homes of a few idiosyncratic telephone collectors (those, like Cheryl, who "think too much"). Some critics have questioned whether Christians can legitimately claim that this rotary telephone is still in working order, or indeed that it ever was. While some of us have gone right on worshiping, praying, and believing, it is important to sketch this debate in outline because it figures so prominently in rediscovering the mystery of God.

Ever since the Enlightenment, science and philosophy have worked in tandem toward the steady elimination of mystery. Much of what passed for mystery in the Middle Ages was correctly revealed as superstition, dispersed like the last wisps of morning mist by the rising sun of reason. René Descartes, the father of modern philosophy, initiated this drive for clarity with his dictum, "As a general rule . . . all things which we *very clearly and distinctly* conceive are true."[10] Diogenes Allen underlines this foundation of modern philosophical thinking: "According to Descartes, everyone's intellect is by nature adequate to perceive truth. Ignorance and error are caused primarily by prejudice produced by custom and sense experience that impede our vision. If one methodically clears them away, the intellect is able to 'see' or intuit the truth, just as the eye can see."[11]

Increasingly in the modern era, philosophy has eschewed its age-old pursuit of wisdom (as its name implies, "love [*phileo*] of wisdom [*sophia*]"). Clarifying the thought process is now philosophy's major goal; analyzing how language may be used has become its primary function. "Mystery will be conceived as arising from two sources: (i) lack of knowledge—it is the business of science to cure this; (ii) unclear thinking—it is the business of philosophy to cure this. The goal toward which both scientist and philosopher are working is a state in which there will be no more mystery."[12] This modern attitude toward mystery has trickled down into the worldviews of many ordinary people, including Christians, convincing them that genuine mystery does not exist.

Questions without Answers

Ludwig Wittgenstein, a twentieth-century philosopher of language, maintained that if there is no meaningful answer, there cannot be a meaningful question: "If a question can be put at all, then it can also be answered. A question can exist only where there is an answer."[13] Wittgenstein summed up his widely influential approach this way: "What can be said at all can be said clearly; and whereof one cannot speak, thereon one must be silent."[14]

We hear echoes of Descartes: only things which we very clearly and distinctly conceive are true. If asking unanswerable questions is meaningless, and the only questions worth asking are those with clear answers, does this not invalidate the mystery of God? The philosophical skepticism of our age also shapes the kinds of questions we Christians ask. How much preaching today might honestly be tagged "Wittgensteinian": asking only those questions to which it knows it already has answers? (For a plea for contrarian preachers not afraid to ask questions with no ready answers, see the afterword.)

However, arguing over what questions can or cannot be asked misses a basic truth we saw in our survey of mystery. God's mystery always comes as a *revelation* to humans, never as an answer to our questions. Human questions never set the agenda in God's revelation; God always takes the initiative. Out of the silence of God's own mystery, God addresses us.

To receive this revelation requires intellectual repentance, says Michael Foster: "Belief in a divine Revelation seems to involve something like a repentance in the sphere of the intellect. . . . When the intellect is faced with God, it must be seized with a conviction of intellectual inadequacy parallel to the moral inadequacy with which we more commonly identify a sense of sin."[15] As we have noted, such a conviction is alien to the typical Western worldview, which inherited from Greek philosophy a belief in the divinity of the intellect. While the Greeks trusted reason as the perfect instrument to discern eternal mystery, it is our admission of intellectual inadequacy that finally puts us in touch with the mystery of God.

How so? Kierkegaard, remember, talked about an "infinite qualitative difference" between Creator and creatures; God is ontologically different from all creation (far more different even than real ducks are from wooden decoys). Thus, no matter how much God graciously reveals to us, God always remains hidden. In response, hopefully our minds come to deeper and deeper appreciation of our conscious ignorance regarding God—we come to know what we do not know. Richard Foster reminds us, "In the very act of hiddenness, God is slowly weaning us of fashioning him in our own image. By refusing to be a puppet on our string or a genie in our bottle, God frees us from our false, idolatrous images."[16]

One example of how we fashion God in our image is believing that being holy (literally "set apart") is something we do *for* God, rather than something God is and does in us. In our pragmatic age, we easily turn holiness into a human achievement, a mastery of technique, something we create in ourselves. Many have decried this state of affairs. Fewer have identified the root of the problem as our loss of the essential mystery of God. Entering the awe-inducing mystery of a holy God saves us from assuming that puny human efforts can somehow replicate holiness in ourselves.

A Mystery We Inhabit

Speaking of the mystery of God, Eugene Peterson maintains, "It is a mystery that we inhabit, not just stand before and ask questions out of curiosity."[17] Our natural first response as we stand before the mystery of God is to ask questions. If biblical paradox is doing its work, it will *prod* us to ask questions, which in turn can stimulate our spiritual imagination and enlarge our worldviews. This is a healthy and essential process. We remember Daniel Migliore's advice as we began this section: "When faith no longer frees people to ask hard questions, it becomes inhuman and dangerous. Unquestioning faith soon slips into ideology, superstition, fanaticism, self-indulgence and idolatry."[18]

Biblical paradoxes are not museum exhibits for us to stroll through, asking the docent an occasional question. No, we *inhabit* them, and as we do, they open us up to God's mystery. We inhabit bodies, with minds and emotions simultaneously wallowing as hippos and soaring like eagles. We are created a little lower than the angels yet are also like the grass that soon passes away. We exist in a saving relationship with

Jesus Christ that is simultaneously God's choice for us and our choice for God. We are shaped by a mandate to extend God's kingdom on earth, even though this kingdom is God's work, not ours. We inhabit the relational being of the three-in-one Father, Son, and Spirit in whose image we are created. We discover a personal God who is incredibly close to us yet transcends this universe so utterly that our minds cannot begin to comprehend how God's being is different from our being. We are centered in "the grace of our Lord Jesus Christ," yet this Jesus Christ who is both divine and human remains absurd to us.

As we inhabit these mysteries, Lesslie Newbigin again forcefully states the case for imagination: "We grow into a knowledge of God by allowing the biblical story to awaken our imagination and to challenge and stimulate our thinking and acting. What we cannot yet understand or accept must nevertheless be allowed to challenge us to more daring thought and commitment. The apophatic tradition in the life of the church is a valid warning to us against supposing that we have all the mystery of the Godhead captured in our theology."[19] Since the early centuries, some Eastern Christians attuned to God's mystery followed the Apophatic Way, a movement that refused to explain God and instead lived in worshipful silence. We are reminded that the word *mystery* itself is derived from the Greek verb *muein*, "close the mouth."[20] A mystery is something before which we close our mouths; we contemplate in wondering silence.[21]

Thus, we reach a point when asking questions—as we have been doing throughout our explorations—invites us into a more profound silence. We begin to inhabit the mystery of God. George Hall gives us an evocative image of paradox as an antechamber to a throne room. The antechamber is filled with much hustle and bustle and chatter, but "after the numbing bewilderment of wrestling with the intractable puzzles which it poses, and after the vertigo of staring into the unfathomableness of its deepest mystery, a gate may open and the chatter become a confused whisper only to give way, by the grace of God, to a silence of a higher order."[22]

Early on, I told a story of pioneers exploring a new land. Game was plentiful, rivers were thick with fish, beauty and majesty beckoned around every bend in the trail. After the challenges and dangers of exploration, creating a settlement was a welcome change for most. Trees were felled, cabins built, crops planted and harvested. Life took on a settled normalcy. The men still hunted and fished, of course, and the women and children often entered the forest to pick berries or look for mushrooms. But fewer trips into the really wild lands were required; the early adventurous days exploring the dark forests and mist-shrouded peaks held wonderful memories, but the pioneers had built homesteads and were busy with the tasks of daily life. While the wilderness still occasionally beckoned, most of the people were now content with what they already knew. The wild lands surrounding their homes were forgotten as they focused on their pragmatic concerns in the small corner of wilderness they had tamed and cultivated.

Similarly, we inhabit the wild, inexhaustible Mystery that is the Father, Son, and Holy Spirit, the Alpha and Omega, the Crucified and Risen One. Yes, we are glad for the settled homesteads where we have cultivated our faith. But we can still venture out to explore the wild and mysterious territory in which we live and move and have our being. Paradox provides ready pathways.

Reflection Questions

1. Where do you see the ideals or goals of pagan magic or Greek mystery still functioning in our world today? How did you react to the descriptions of these two kinds of mystery?

2. What, if anything, in the biblical overview of mystery surprised you or challenged you?

3. Do you agree that the Western philosophical worldview has made the essential hiddenness or mystery of God hard even for Christians to accept today?

4. How do you respond to the idea that we inhabit the mystery of God?

EPILOGUE

The Duke Humfrey Library

> *We shall not cease from exploration*
> *And the end of all our exploring*
> *Will be to arrive where we started*
> *And know the place for the first time.*
> —T. S. Eliot, "Little Gidding"

We began with Cheryl's letter and ended with the crab shell of worldview. As we grow spiritually, we move out of one worldview so we might move into another, one that encompasses more of God. This is what Cheryl did. A paradoxical question stimulated her imagination and became a good problem for her. Despite the advice of her friends to let go of her problem, exploring it for Cheryl generated a "strange sort of comfort" in discovering a far larger (and yet more mysterious) God. Our imagination often prods us toward such growth; one of the tools it uses is paradox.

Paradox stimulates our imagination to see faith in fresh ways, not as certainty but as an ever-expanding synthesis of knowledge and trust. Like the twin tines of a tuning fork, knowledge and trust remain in harmonic tension, vibrating in unison, constantly correcting each other. Insisting on certainty is the shell some of us need to vacate; then our faith can begin growing again.

Paradox stimulates our imagination to see faith and reason as dance partners, each taking turns leading or following as faith seeks understanding. Freezing faith and reason in a static relationship is the shell some of us need to leave behind; then we can allow our faith and reason to freely complement one another in more nuanced ways.

195

Paradox stimulates our imagination by bringing the complexities of life and faith front and center so we cannot ignore them. This serves us well in two ways: first, we are more realistic and can refuse to settle for a simplicity that does not acknowledge complexity; second, as we journey into the complexity, we hope to arrive at a more profound simplicity on the other side. Being satisfied with easy answers and simple formulas is the shell some of us need to move beyond; then we can discover a deeper and richer Christian hope.

Paradox stimulates our imagination to explore the mystery of God as a realm we inhabit. We have built homesteads and cultivated small corners of this wild landscape, but the mystery of God is still all around us! Exploring paradox gets us asking questions and moving deeper into the mystery, but eventually we reach a point where we rest in God's mystery without needing to figure it out. As Cheryl finally concluded, "there is a God and I am not he." Expecting to have all our questions answered is the shell some of us need to put behind us; then we can rest in the mystery of God.

As paradox stimulates our imagination in these and other ways, we may experience the second-order change we met with the seriously playful paradoxes of Jesus: "Second-order solutions are often viewed from within the system as unpredictable, amazing, and surprising, since they are not necessarily based on the rules and assumptions of that system."[1] One of paradox's most valuable gifts is injecting new thoughts and opportunities for growth into what can become closed systems (or worldviews).

Keith Webb describes driving on backcountry roads through beautiful French countryside; frequently stuck behind farm tractors on narrow, winding roads, he traveled slowly. His GPS told him he was still three hours away from his destination and thus late for an appointment. Rather than responding in a typical American way (a tighter grip on the steering wheel, straining to press ahead), he stopped for coffee and a croissant. When he started his car again, the GPS automatically reset itself and he immediately noticed it was set to avoid toll roads. A simple reprogramming of the GPS to include toll roads instantly offered a new route that was two hours faster.[2] Second-order change intervenes from outside our systems.

Our worldview is an internal GPS system guiding us through life. From inside our worldview, we easily assume our only options are making small adjustments or trying harder. Outside intervention resets our worldview to incorporate more of reality (toll roads) that we would otherwise miss—such is the second-order change that biblical paradox stimulates through our imagination. Expanding our worldview is often a wonderful gift.

═══════════

As I write these words, I gaze across study tables in the thirteenth-century Duke Humfrey Library, the oldest section of Oxford University's Bodleian Library. Mahogany-paneled walls and bookshelves surround me, illuminated to a burnished glow by leaded-glass windows set in stone traceries. Stained-glass crests within the windows sparkle in the morning sun. Thirty feet above me, brightly painted heraldic shields of forgotten nobles add color between the dark oak rafters of the hammer-beam ceiling. Portraits of fourteenth- and fifteenth-century clerics on the whitewashed walls stare impassively down at me.

To reach my desk, I walk past readers poring over medieval manuscripts by the soft light of reading lamps. Dusty, leather-bound volumes are stacked helter-skelter on groaning wooden shelves above their heads. Some readers sit hunched over huge parchments written in Greek and Latin, while others inspect pocket-size books with magnifying glasses, and still others clack away on laptops, translating as they read.

I ponder their intense concentration. Why do they spend their days closeted here, when they could be basking in the English sunshine? What secrets do these ancient books hold for them? Are they simply completing a thesis on some arcane topic so they can get on with the rest of their lives? Or is there some deeper attraction?

Even though my work requires no ancient manuscripts, I keep returning to this magical place. I love the smell of learning, the sensation of being surrounded by the wisdom of the ages. If I close my eyes, I feel as if I might easily open them again to find medieval monks copying ancient texts for posterity. Little has changed from the days when only clerics populated this repository of human knowledge.

Then it hits me: one day this place will disappear. It may not be the fire that consumed the library of the ancients at Alexandria, nor perhaps human negligence or some natural disaster. Will these books that have been tenderly shepherded for centuries disappear in a flash of brilliance at the final consummation (Mark 13:31)? The humanist in me pales at the prospect. The creation to which we Christians look forward is a new heaven and earth, but still a material one with rivers and trees, cities and thrones. Who is to say how much human culture will carry over into it?

The whine of electric saws interrupts my reverie. Workmen hammer away, shoring up portions of the sacred shelves where termites as well as scholars have been at work. It is just wood, I remind myself. I glance at the book title at eye level next to me: *Norfolk and Norwich Archaeological Society, Middlesex County Record, Wills at Chester 1545 to 1620.* Well, perhaps not *all* the books are priceless classics! Could much of this library, I ruefully wonder, simply be the dusty attic of Great Britain?

These whiffs of disillusionment remind me of the glaring contrast on my first day in this august environment. Frequent cries of "All quiet!" echoed up through the open lead-paned windows. The demands for silence were not from intense scholars but from the movie set of *Gulliver's Travels*, which was being filmed one floor beneath me. Such is paradox.

Paradox is the Duke Humfrey Library. When this place has served its purpose, we might little mourn its passing in the joy of finally knowing as we have been known. "For now we see through a glass, darkly; but then face to face: now I know in part; but then shall I know even as also I am known" (1 Cor. 13:12 KJV).

For now, paradox is part of our human struggle to see more clearly and know more deeply. When we encounter God face-to-face, will the biblical paradoxes that offer glimpses into the mystery of God disappear? Will the great ontological divide that separates us from God disappear with them? Perhaps paradox will have served its purpose. Or perhaps some of these paradoxes will remain, or new ones take their place. God's mystery may still be beyond our comprehension. All this remains to be seen. In the meantime, paradox is waiting to guide us as we dimly peer through the glass.

AFTERWORD

A Plea for Contrarian Preachers (and Listeners)

> *I, yet not I, but Christ.*
> —Paul

During my seminary years, I worked as a Young Life leader to finance my education and develop skill in relational ministry. I quickly realized that my introverted temperament (let's face it, I was dull) was not typical for Young Life leaders. My first day on the job, another male leader and I walked into a high school cafeteria during lunch hour. A bevy of sophomore girls soon flocked around him. Indicating me, he said, "Oh, this is Rich, one of our new leaders." A few girls shot me quick, sidelong glances before turning back to him. That day I knew this was not going to be easy! At my first Young Life club meeting, hosted in a home later that week, I planned to fade into the background until I felt more comfortable. In a living room packed with kids, I was sitting out of the way on a windowsill and leaned back so far that I shattered the windowpane! The splintering crash riveted all eyes on me: "Oh, this is Rich, one of our new leaders."

Trying not to appear awkward as I felt nothing *but* awkward, I spent that first year slowly and painfully learning the art of meeting kids on their own turf. My fellow leaders thought I was cute in a bumbling sort of way, the Phil Dunphy (*Modern Family*) or Don Knotts (*Andy Griffith Show*) of Young Life leaders!

My second year brought a new assignment that would have challenged a veteran. All by myself, I would pioneer a new club in an Episcopalian college-prep high school that catered to the social upper crust across a large metropolitan area. The students were very bright, very rich, and *very* self-assured. I plunged in, however, and after a few months actually organized a functioning club which some kids attended regularly. One was Greg, a lanky, sensitive boy who, like lots of others at this prestigious school, had parents whose other priorities outdistanced their sixteen-year-old. One Saturday night in January while his parents were away, Greg hanged himself from a basement water pipe.

A few days later, I found myself speaking about Greg's suicide to the entire student body. Chapel services functioned mostly as assemblies; explicitly Christian content was closely monitored so as not to offend students of other faiths. As I drove to school that cold morning, I wondered what in the world had possessed me to volunteer to speak. What I thought would be a strategic opportunity to offer a witness for Christ now looked like social suicide. Some of the faculty were already skeptical, if not hostile, toward Christianity in general and my presence on campus in particular. I was there only because a few wealthy families too influential to refuse wanted the school exposed to Young Life. I had no experience in speaking before large groups. I wondered if anything I planned to say even made sense. The moment came and, rubbing my sweaty palms together, I walked to the center of the chapel platform without my notes. I talked about how life can peel us like an onion until we get to the very center. Somehow Greg's center did not hold. None of us would ever know why. It remained for us to think about the center of our own lives. For me, I went on, I had discovered that Jesus Christ offers the center I needed.

As I spoke to the students, they sat attentively. After chapel, student after student came up to thank me for my "great talk." Faculty members smiled and complimented me as well. The affirmation continued in the cafeteria during lunch hour, often from students I didn't know. If only for a moment, a nerve had been touched. The gospel had penetrated many who would normally not give the gospel, or me, the time of day.

Yet as clearly as I have ever known anything in my life, I knew it was "I, yet not I, but Christ."

My spine still tingles as I recall this experience thirty-five years ago in that high school auditorium. God spoke through *my* words. I have felt it many times since, whenever God has encountered others through my preaching. But seldom, if ever, has the distance been so vast between the inadequacy I felt and the reaction I witnessed.

The Paradox of Preaching

Most preachers will tell a similar story. "They were my words, yet people heard Jesus through them!" This is the paradox of preaching. It is the wild territory of "I, yet not I, but Christ." Preaching that is only my words is dead on arrival in the ears of my people. Yet I must not disparage my words, because they are the only words Jesus has to use. If God's Word is going to be proclaimed on that particular day in that particular place, it *will* be through the words my mind and heart create and my voice articulates.

Preaching is a paradox. A preacher with ugly thoughts about a contentious elder in the third row can step up to a pulpit and find his or her stumbling words transformed into the word of God, the same word thundered from Mount Sinai or whispered in a still, small voice, the same word proclaimed by prophets and apostles, the same word revealed incarnate in Jesus Christ. The Second Helvetic Confession proclaims, "Preaching the Word of God is the Word of God."[1] I vividly remember the shock, actually something closer to panic, that this confessional statement first prompted in me. I did not mind if God zapped my sermons to give them extra punch. In fact, I prayed regularly for this to happen. However, to consider that every time I stand up to preach, the very word of God might somehow come forth from my mouth was (and still is) a dizzying proposition!

What we have in view is *preaching*, not individual sermons. Even this lofty a view of preaching is not carte blanche. While I believe preaching is indeed incarnational, it is not transubstantiation. No assurance is

given that every word becomes the word of God. No formulas or pro-
cedures, no fail-safe methods of preparation, no techniques followed
with scrupulous intensity guarantee it will happen. Preaching remains a
mystery, perhaps most of all to its practitioners. Formulas can produce
entertaining talks which keep people smiling and appreciative; the
word of God is beyond any human control. "The wind blows wherever
it pleases" (John 3:8).

Scottish theologian Donald Baillie, in his monumental *God Was in
Christ*, writes about a similar paradox. Christian people give credit to
God for the good they do, yet ascribing all to God in no way abrogates
personal responsibility: "Never is human action more truly and fully
personal, never does the agent feel more perfectly free, than in those
moments of which he can say as a Christian that whatever good was in
them was not his but God's."[2]

Many of us have witnessed this paradox. We expend enormous
effort, yet feel a profound sense that we deserve no credit: "I, yet not
I, but Christ." Baillie moves on to analyze how an action can simultaneously be the result of human effort and divine grace: "It is not as
though we could divide the honours between God and ourselves, God
doing his part and we doing ours. It is false to this paradox to think of
the area of God's action and the area of human action being delimited,
each by the other, and distinguished from each other by a boundary, so
that the more of God's grace there is in my action, the less there is of
my own personal action."[3]

A Pentecostal preacher once told me that he never worked on his
sermons in advance because it quenched the Spirit. As I understood
him, his human thoughts would get in the way of the pure word con-
veyed by the Spirit. For him, Donald Baillie's boundary between what
we do and what God does was clear: he had little to do but let his
mouth be God's vessel. Such a view seems to give the Lord all the credit
but actually diminishes God's power and majesty. The Holy Spirit is
reduced to a Western Union operator, transmitting his message over
fragile wires that can barely be trusted. This hardly squares with the
God of the Bible, who never "channeled" his messages but spoke to
the secret hearts of prophets and apostles and, in the mystery of divine

grace, trusted these fallible, earthen vessels to deliver his word with power and authority.

Too often, however, our working theology becomes, "I do my part and hope God does his part." But where does my part end and God's part begin? Is it the moment when I am delivering the sermon? Receiving insight while grappling with a biblical text in the study? Saving a germinal idea gleaned from a newspaper article? Or is it even earlier, perhaps a youthful experience that set the stage for a significant sermon many years later? Perhaps God was working on my sermons long before I knew I would be a preacher. Preaching is rife with paradox and mystery.

Bill Gates's Sunday Morning

The key question skeptics used to ask about Christianity was, Is it true? The question asked from many quarters today is, Does it work? When asked why he does not attend a church, Bill Gates replied, "Just in terms of allocation of time resources, religion is not very efficient. There's a lot more I could be doing on a Sunday morning."[4] Churches everywhere promise consumer-minded prospects like Bill Gates big dividends for their time investment: "Join Us This Sunday and Your Life Will Never Be the Same!"

Preachers become vendors in this spiritual street market, each hawking their wares to shoppers who pause for just a moment before strolling on to the next booth. With such a small window of opportunity, sermons must hit felt needs quickly. They must cut to the chase, get down to basics, offer spiritual principles and practical handles that match people's expectations.

I certainly have done my share of catering to the marketplace. But when will I tackle the large chunks of life of little interest to the market? When will I speak to issues that are *not* practical? When will I address needs that are *not* felt? Can I raise questions that have no answers (at least, no easy answers)? But who wants to hear about those confusing, contradictory, or incomprehensible parts of faith most of us wish to ignore or forget? And what preacher in his or her right mind raises *more* thorny issues to consumers looking for ways to remove the burrs already under their saddles?

Describing the anti-intellectualism of American revivalism, historian John Jefferson Davis writes, "A pragmatic America and a frenetic frontier asked of the sermon only that it work."[5] *Pragmatism* is often our byword today. Truth is important, of course, but please let it be *practical* truth that works in my daily life.

I wooed people with practical answers to felt needs for years before I realized I was not really helping them with their basic need: to know God. To my chagrin, just the opposite happened! The pressure to have all the answers not only shrinks the spiritual imagination of both communicators and listeners but stifles wholesome faith. I was peddling a God who was too small, a problem-solving God instead of the awesomely mysterious God of Abraham, Isaac, and Jacob. The God whom Moses meets in thunder and fire on Mount Sinai is too quickly replaced by a golden calf, "a god without mystery, a god who was there when they needed it."[6]

Of course, becoming a disciple of Jesus has positive lifestyle implications. (God does meet our felt needs.) But the biblical goal is never to improve people's lives. It is, rather, "that they *know* you, the only true God, and Jesus Christ, whom you have sent" (John 17:3, emphasis added). "Obviously Christ's teaching is therapeutic and restorative," evangelist Ravi Zacharias notes. "But Christ's teaching is therapeutic because it's *true*."[7]

While sermons addressing biblical paradox do not "work" in a pragmatic, results-oriented sense, I have argued that paradox does contribute to a maturing life of faith. It offers a reality check, reminding us that God is greater than we will ever comprehend (Isa. 55:8–9). We tend to forget this in a culture where the highest good is getting things done, with God too often just another technology to make our lives a little better. As the stock market has contrarian investors who invest against the direction the market is trending, today the spiritual marketplace in contemporary America calls for contrarian preachers.

The Need for Contrarian Preachers (and Listeners)

My journey as a developing preacher can be described as carving a home in the wilderness. At first, all was new and exotic, a great adventure. An adrenaline-pumping immediacy of staying alive from one Sunday to the next was itself a challenge. New discoveries were around every bend in the trail. Portions of wilderness that looked forbidding when I first arrived were cleared. Habits of study and preparation were formed, styles of delivery developed. While I retained the memory of what this land was like when I first arrived—all wild and menacing and unknown—I had settled in and built a homestead.

This itself is a paradox, for those most alive to the nuances and potentialities of preaching are at home, yet not at home. They know the lay of the land, how to maneuver and get around; yet they have not lost their thirst for the unknown. They dwell in the security of the homestead yet get away when they can to tramp the still-unexplored hills and valleys.

Why is this? Perhaps they realize there is *so* much, both dangerous and glorious, still out there waiting for them. Perhaps they realize that it is *all* still wilderness, even the cultivated, built-up parts, in the sense that they cannot control or subdue or package any of it. All they can do is live in it. Living there is a wonderful, holy privilege.

Here is my contention: human life, Christian faith, and honest preaching are all shot through with paradox, not in a way that makes them meaningless but in a way that gives them meaning beyond our comprehension and control. We started this exploration into paradox with Roger Hazelton's contention: "Faith is like a forest which urges us on and deepens, even as it corrects and satisfies, our thought. By its means we never know God and ourselves wholly, yet we know nevertheless truly. We may see in a glass darkly, but we really do see."[8] This is a manifesto for contrarian preachers!

When we preach into the wilder regions of faith, listeners will rejoice that their preacher is wrestling with issues that deeply perplex them; even if through a glass darkly, they really do see. Preachers will rejoice that they are leading their people deeper into the mystery of knowing God and themselves better—truly, if not wholly.

Contrarian preachers (and listeners) must push back against the pervasive, if often unconscious, desire for a pragmatic god who meets our needs. Contrarian preachers (and listeners) must defend the rationality of their faith but reject any reductionism that drains their faith of its inherent mystery. Contrarian preachers must equip contrarian listeners to discern between absurdity and mystery, confident that genuine mystery lingers on, like glittering crystals after the liquid has evaporated. Contrarian preachers and listeners must stimulate each other's imagination, hoping that their biblical worldview will grow as well.

We are not adequate for these tasks by ourselves. Contrarian preachers and contrarian listeners need to find one another and encourage one another. Together, they can occasionally leave the familiar homestead behind and take field trips to where their spiritual ancestors encountered God's mystery.

Reflection Questions

1. Have you ever had an experience, as when the author spoke to the high school students, where you absolutely *knew* that God was at work?

2. Do you agree that preaching is a paradox? Why or why not?

3. If you are a preacher or teacher, what in this book might be useful as you proclaim the whole counsel of God?

4. If you listen to sermons, what in this book might help you to listen better (or to encourage your preacher)?

APPENDIX

Three Orders of Paradox

	1. Serious Playfulness	2. Tuning Fork	3. Two Handles
Key Image	Picture Frame: reframes reality as we look through it	Tuning Fork: both tines must vibrate together to create a new note	Auger: performs best when hands are far apart on opposite handles
Characteristic Tension	Startles us but ultimately dissolves	Keeps polarities in vibration together	Keeps both sides of the paradox separate and distinct
Representative Examples	• Sayings of Jesus • Parables of the kingdom[a] • Great reversals[b] • Faith versus works	• Justice/love • Transcendent/personal • Election/free will • God's kingdom	• Humanity • Scripture • Trinity • Jesus Christ
What do we see as we look through it?	Mystery of life in God's kingdom	Mystery of God's relationship with us, and ours with God	Mystery of God's being and our own being
Strategies for Preaching	• Narratives/stories • Playfulness • Allow listeners to connect the dots on their own	• Present two ideas vibrating back and forth ("C . . . Ar")	• Don't try to reconcile opposing ideas • Employ Pascal's "vaunt/abase" style
Risk to Avoid	Trying too hard	Giving one side more attention, which stifles their tension and obscures their harmony	Allowing the stark black and white opposites to coalesce into a dirty gray

[a] Parables of the kingdom (e.g., Matt. 13:24–30, 31–32, 33, 44–46, 47–50).
[b] Great reversals (e.g., Mark 9:35; 12:10; Matt. 20:1–16; Mark 9:40; Matt. 12:30; 25:29).

NOTES

Chapter 1: A Strange Sort of Comfort

1. Gordon Graham, "Mystery or Mumbo-Jumbo?" *Philosophical Investigations* 7 (October 1984): 284ff.
2. Aleksandr Solzhenitsyn, *The Gulag Archipelago 1918–1956*, *https://www .goodreads.com/work/quotes/2944012–1918–1956* (accessed November 2014).
3. David Brooks, "What Candidates Need," *New York Times*, April 6, 2015.
4. A. W. Tozer, "The Works of A. W. Tozer," *Daily Christian Quote*, *http:// dailychristianquote.com/dcqchristianliving8.html* (accessed November 2013).
5. Miroslav Volf, *Exclusion and Embrace: A Theological Exploration of Identity, Otherness and Reconciliation* (Nashville: Abingdon, 1996), 9.
6. Ibid.
7. John H. Leith, *Basic Christian Doctrine* (Louisville: Westminster/John Knox, 1993), 25–27. Several differences between problems and mystery are drawn from Leith's discussion.
8. Ibid.
9. James W. Sire, *The Universe Next Door*, 5th ed. (Downers Grove, Ill.: InterVarsity, 2009), 166ff. Sire offers an excellent summary of the New Age pursuit of mystery in his chapter "A Separate Universe: The New Age— Spirituality without Religion."
10. John R. W. Stott, *The Contemporary Christian* (Leicester: Inter-Varsity, 1992), 223.
11. Quoted in Diogenes Allen, *Philosophy for Understanding Theology* (Atlanta: John Knox Press, 1985), 289. Allen points out that while twentieth-century skeptics saw Wittgenstein as an ally, he actually believed that there is more to reality than can be expressed through human words.
12. Antoine de Saint-Exupéry, *www.goodreads.com/quotes/232915-the-author -who-benefits-you-most-is-not-the-one* (accessed August 2015).

Chapter 2: Fog

1. E. L. Mascall, *Words and Images* (New York: Longmans, Green, and Co., 1957), 78–79.

2. Ibid., 39.

3. Roger Hazelton, "The Nature of Christian Paradox," *Theology Today* 6 (October 1949): 44.

4. Friedrich von Hügel, *The Reality of God* (London: Dent, 1931), 187.

5. John Macquarrie, *Thinking about God* (London: SCM Press, 1975), 33.

6. John Leith, *Basic Christian Doctrine* (Louisville: Westminster John Knox, 1993), 24.

7. Karl Barth, *Church Dogmatics*, II/1, ed. G. W. Bromiley and T. F. Torrance (Edinburgh: T. and T. Clark, 1957), 179ff.

8. Eugene Peterson, *Tell It Slant: A Conversation on the Language of Jesus in His Stories and Prayers* (Grand Rapids, Mich.: Eerdmans, 2008), 128.

9. Barth, *Church Dogmatics*, 423.

10. Hazelton, "Nature of Christian Paradox," 44.

Chapter 3: Newton's Apple

1. Fritz Rohrlich, *From Paradox to Reality: Our New Concepts of the Physical World* (New York: Cambridge Univ. Press, 1987), 114. "In all these cases the superseded model was not 'wrong.' It was simply found to be valid only in a much smaller domain of validity than was originally thought. In the same way, Newtonian mechanics is not 'wrong' just because we know about special relativity. It is just not a good enough approximation and is therefore restricted to a smaller domain of validity than was previously thought."

2. Ibid., 143–44.

3. Thomas Kuhn, *Metaphor, Paradox, and Paradigm: The Structure of Scientific Revolutions* (Chicago: Univ. of Chicago Press, 1970). Kuhn ushered the phrase "paradigm shift" into our everyday vocabulary. How often do we blithely speak of paradigm shifts today, not realizing the idea came from identifying the central role paradox plays in changing scientific worldviews? As with the wave/particle paradox, again and again paradox has brought scientists to the limits of human perception, to "think about that about which we cannot think."

4. Rohrlich, *From Paradox to Reality*, 7. "[A]ll levels of reality are equally true. They just describe different approximations. Each level presents features of reality not found on other levels. For example, atomic physics tells us nothing about the nature of life which we learn from the study of living organisms. . . . [O]nly when all levels are considered together, i.e., when we have before us nature in all approximations, do we obtain a complete picture or at least a picture as complete as present-day science would admit."

5. Jeffrey Astley, "Paradox and Christology," *King's Theological Review* 7 (Spring 1984): 9–13. Astley reviews several attempts to use the wave/particle duality, as well as indicates some of its limitations for theology.

6. James Gleick, *Chaos: Making a New Science* (New York: Penguin, 2008), 68.

Chapter 4: Serious Playfulness

1. Robert H. Stein, *The Method and Message of Jesus' Teaching* (Philadelphia: Westminster Press, 1978), 19–20.
2. Gordon Graham, "Mystery or Mumbo-Jumbo?" *Philosophical Investigations* 7 (October 1984): 284ff.
3. Viktor E. Frankl, "Paradoxical Intention and Dereflection," *Psychotherapy: Theory, Research and Practice* 12, no. 3 (Fall 1975): 226.
4. Paul Deschenes and Vance L. Shepperson, "The Ethics of Paradox," *Journal of Psychology and Theology* 11 (Summer 1983): 92.
5. Ibid., 97.
6. Dennis D. Morgan, Dale H. Levandowski, and Martha L. Rogers, "The Apostle Paul: Problem Formation and Problem Resolution from a Systems Perspective," *Journal of Psychology and Theology* 9, no. 2 (Summer 1981): 136–43. Descriptions and examples of first- and second-order change are taken from this article.
7. L. Michael Ascher, "Paradoxical Intention and Recursive Anxiety," in *Therapeutic Paradox*, ed. L. Michael Ascher (New York: Guilford Press, 1989), 108.
8. L. Michael Ascher, "Therapeutic Paradox: A Primer," in Ascher, *Therapeutic Paradox*, 6.
9. Elton Trueblood, *The Humor of Christ* (New York: Harper and Row, 1964), 47.
10. Stein, *Method and Message*, 20.
11. There are also exceptions outside the Gospels, however. Consider *"Continue to work out your salvation* with fear and trembling, for it is *God who works in you to will and to act in order to fulfill his good purpose"* (Phil. 2:12–13, emphasis added) and "The *Word* became *flesh"* (John 1:14, emphasis added).

Chapter 5: Try Harder!

1. L. Michael Ascher, "Paradoxical Intention and Recursive Anxiety," in *Therapeutic Paradox*, ed. L. Michael Ascher (New York: Guilford Press, 1989), 108.
2. L. Michael Ascher, "Therapeutic Paradox: A Primer," in Ascher, *Therapeutic Paradox*, 7.
3. Dennis D. Morgan, Dale H. Levandowski, and Martha L. Rogers, "The Apostle Paul: Problem Formation and Problem Resolution from a Systems Perspective," *Journal of Psychology and Theology* 9, no. 2 (Summer 1981): 136–43.
4. Edwin H. Friedman, *Generation to Generation: Family Process in Church and Synagogue* (New York: Guilford Press, 1985), 50: "Seriousness is more than an attitude; it is a total orientation, a way of thinking embedded

in constant, chronic anxiety. It is characterized by lack of flexibility in response, a narrow repertoire of approaches, persistent efforts to try harder, an inability to change direction. . . ."

5. Ibid., 51.

6. Ibid.

7. Ibid., 205–7.

8. Brendan Nyhan, "When Beliefs and Facts Collide," *New York Times*, July 7, 2014, *http://www.nytimes.com/2014/07/06/upshot/when-beliefs-and-facts -collide.html?src=xps&abt=0002&abg=0.*

9. Friedman, *Generation to Generation*, 52.

10. Ibid., 208–10.

11. Viktor E. Frankl, "Paradoxical Intention and Dereflection," *Psychotherapy: Theory, Research and Practice* 12, no. 3 (Fall 1975): 228.

12. *Matthew*, DVD, directed by Reghardt van den Bergh (Visual Bible, 1997).

13. Elton Trueblood, *The Humor of Christ* (New York: Harper and Row, 1964), 46–47.

14. Ibid.

15. Ibid., 59.

Chapter 6: New Frames

1. Mark Twain, *The Adventures of Tom Sawyer* (New York: Penguin, 1986), 22.

2. Ibid.

3. Paul Deschenes and Vance L. Shepperson, "The Ethics of Paradox," *Journal of Psychology and Theology* 11 (Summer 1983): 93.

4. Edwin H. Friedman, *Generation to Generation: Family Process in Church and Synagogue* (New York: Guilford Press, 1985), 11–12.

5. Deschenes and Shepperson, "Ethics of Paradox," 93.

6. Dennis D. Morgan, Dale H. Levandowski, and Martha L. Rogers, "The Apostle Paul: Problem Formation and Problem Resolution from a Systems Perspective," *Journal of Psychology and Theology* 9, no. 2 (Summer 1981): 136–43.

7. Lesslie Newbigin, *Proper Confidence: Faith, Doubt and Certainty in Christian Discipleship* (Grand Rapids, Mich.: Eerdmans, 1995), 38–39.

8. See Fred Craddock, *As One without Authority*, 3rd ed. (Nashville: Abingdon, 1981), for one of the earliest but still one of the best arguments for the inductive style so common in Jesus' preaching.

9. Eugene Peterson, *Tell It Slant: A Conversation on the Language of Jesus in His Stories and Prayers* (Grand Rapids, Mich.: Eerdmans, 2008), 59–60.

10. Ibid., 31.

Chapter 7: Terror and Truth on Flight 451

1. Eugene Peterson, *Tell It Slant: A Conversation on the Language of Jesus in His Stories and Prayers* (Grand Rapids, Mich.: Eerdmans, 2008), 134.

Chapter 8: Pavlov's Dogs

1. Eric J. Cohen, "Induced Christian Neurosis: An Examination of Pragmatic Paradoxes and the Christian Faith," *Journal of Psychology and Theology* 10 (Spring 1982): 5–12. This article describes Pavlov's experiment and the three distinguishing criteria of the double bind.
2. Dan Greenberg, *How to Be a Jewish Mother* (Los Angeles: Price/Stern/Sloan, 1964), 16.
3. Cohen, "Induced Christian Neurosis," 11.
4. Dennis D. Morgan, Dale H. Levandowski, and Martha L. Rogers, "The Apostle Paul: Problem Formation and Problem Resolution from a Systems Perspective," *Journal of Psychology and Theology* 9, no. 2 (Summer 1981): 143.

Chapter 9: The Tuning Fork

1. L. M. Montgomery, *Emily of the New Moon* (London: George G. Harrap, 1928), 6.
2. Ibid.
3. Jimmy Chin interview, March 7, 2015, True/False Film Festival, Columbia, Mo.
4. Rudolf Otto, *The Idea of the Holy: An Inquiry into the Non-rational Factor in the Idea of the Divine and Its Relation to the Rational*, 2nd ed., trans. John W. Harvey (London: Oxford Univ. Press, 1950), 12–40.
5. Paul S. Fiddes, *Freedom and Limit: A Dialogue between Literature and Christian Doctrine* (Macon: Mercer Univ. Press, 1999), 6.
6. Ibid., 10.
7. Hugh Evan Hopkins, *Charles Simeon of Cambridge* (London: Hodder and Stoughton, 1977), 38.
8. Ibid., 177.
9. Ibid., 76.

Chapter 10: 'Course He Isn't Safe . . . but He's Good

1. C. S. Lewis, *The Lion, the Witch and the Wardrobe* (New York: HarperCollins, 1950), 79–80.
2. A. W. Tozer, *The Knowledge of the Holy* (San Francisco: Harper and Row, 1961), 1.
3. Ibid., 89.

4. C. S. Lewis, *Mere Christianity* (New York: Simon and Schuster, 1943), 38.

5. C. S. Lewis, *The Problem of Pain* (New York: HarperCollins, 2001), 46–47.

Chapter 11: Now My Eyes See

1. Diogenes Allen, *Philosophy for Understanding Theology* (Atlanta: John Knox Press, 1985), 2.

2. Carl Sagan, *The Varieties of Scientific Experience: A Personal View of the Search for God* (New York: Penguin, 2006), 6.

3. William P. Alston, *Divine Nature and Human Language: Essays in Philosophical Theology* (Ithaca, N.Y.: Cornell Univ. Press, 1989), 147.

4. Karen Armstrong, *A History of God* (New York: Alfred Knopf, 1993), 387.

5. Ibid., 396.

6. Ibid., 438, 446.

7. Ibid., 438.

8. Ibid.

9. Ibid., 454.

10. Ibid.

11. Donald McCullough, *The Trivialization of God* (Colorado Springs: NavPress, 1995), 13–26. McCullough offers an excellent discussion of the ways mystery has been drained out of modern "trivial gods."

Chapter 12: Who Chooses First?

1. Richard Foster, *Money, Sex and Power: The Challenge of the Disciplined Life* (San Francisco: Harper and Row, 1985), 20.

2. D. A. Carson, *Divine Sovereignty and Human Responsibility: Biblical Perspectives in Tension* (Grand Rapids, Mich.: Baker Book House; London: Marshall Pickering, 1994), 220.

3. Ibid.

4. Steven D. Boyer and Christopher A. Hall, *The Mystery of God: Theology for Knowing the Unknowable* (Grand Rapids, Mich.: Baker Academic, 2012), 167. I am indebted to Boyer and Hall for the ideas expressed in this paragraph. See pp. 166–71.

5. Ibid., 171. See the chapter "Mystery and Salvation," pp. 147–75, for a thoughtful discussion about how God's mystery transforms this "election/ free will" debate, especially pp. 173–75 for helpful pastoral responses to people struggling with this issue from both the Calvinist and Arminian positions.

Chapter 13: Already . . . Not Yet

1. Abraham Kuyper, *www.goodreads.com/author/quotes/385896.Abraham_Kuyper* (accessed November 2014).
2. George Ladd, *A Theology of the New Testament* (Grand Rapids, Mich.: Eerdmans, 1974), 94. Much has been written on the nature of parables that hide and yet simultaneously reveal, especially in regard to the mystery of the kingdom.
3. Gordon Fee, *The First Epistle to the Corinthians* (Grand Rapids, Mich.: Eerdmans, 1987), 17.
4. Eugene Peterson, *Tell It Slant: A Conversation on the Language of Jesus in His Stories and Prayers* (Grand Rapids, Mich.: Eerdmans, 2008), 175.
5. Parker Palmer, *The Promise of Paradox: A Celebration of Contradictions in the Christian Life* (San Francisco: Jossey-Bass, 1980), 63.
6. Ibid., xxix.

Chapter 14: The Two Handles

1. G. K. Chesterton, *Orthodoxy* (Garden City, N.Y.: Image, 1959), 100.
2. Ibid.
3. Ibid.
4. Ibid., 97.

Chapter 15: Eagles and Hippos

1. Francis S. Collins, *The Language of God: A Scientist Presents Evidence for Belief* (New York: Free Press, 2006), 137.
2. See my article "Transforming the Dualistic Worldview of Ethiopian Evangelical Christians," *International Bulletin of Missionary Research* (July 2015), 138–41.
3. Blaise Pascal, *Pensées*, trans. W. F. Trotter (New York: E. P. Dutton and Co., 1958), 97.
4. Stanley J. Grenz, *Theology for the Community of God* (Grand Rapids, Mich.: Eerdmans, 2000), 131–32.
5. Nancey Murphy, *Bodies and Souls or Spirited Bodies?* (Cambridge: Cambridge Univ. Press, 2006), 59–61. See also Robert Wright, "Can Machines Think?" *Time* (March 25, 1996), 50–56.
6. Eugene Peterson, *Christ Plays in Ten Thousand Places: A Conversation in Spiritual Theology* (Grand Rapids, Mich.: Eerdmans, 2005), 79.
7. Barry Schwartz, *The Paradox of Choice: Why More Is Less* (San Francisco: HarperCollins, 2009), 15.
8. Jim Sollisch, "Paradox of Modern Life: So Many Choices, So Little Joy," May 20, 2011, *Christian Science Monitor*, *www.csmonitor.com/Commentary/*

Opinion/2011/0520/Paradox-of-modern-life-so-many-choices-so-little-joy
(accessed November 2013).

9. Pascal, *Pensées*, 130.

10. Paul Tournier, *The Seasons of Life* (London: SCM Press, 1964), 11–12.

11. Ayn Rand, *The Fountainhead* (New York: Plume, 1994).

12. G. K. Chesterton, *Orthodoxy* (Garden City, N.Y.: Image, 1959), 94.

13. C. S. Lewis, *A Mind Awake: An Anthology of C. S. Lewis*, ed. Clyde S. Kilby (New York: Harvest/HBJ, 1968), 21.

14. Gerhard von Rad, *Genesis* (Philadelphia: Westminster Press, 1972), 169.

15. F. Dale Bruner, *Matthew*, vol. 2 (Dallas: Word, 1990), 588.

16. Quoted in Elton Trueblood, *The Humor of Christ* (New York: Harper and Row, 1964), 74.

17. Thomas Merton, *A Thomas Merton Reader*, ed. Thomas P. McDonnell (New York: Doubleday, 1989), 16.

18. Ibid.

19. Chesterton, *Orthodoxy*, 94.

20. C. S. Lewis, *Miracles: A Preliminary Study* (New York: Touchstone, 1996), 145.

Chapter 16: Treasure and Vessel

1. G. C. Berkouwer, *Holy Scripture* (Grand Rapids, Mich.: Eerdmans, 1975), 207.

2. Ibid.

3. Fred Craddock, *As One without Authority*, 3rd ed. (Nashville: Abingdon, 1981), 41.

4. Arthur F. Holmes, *Faith Seeks Understanding: A Christian Approach to Knowledge* (Grand Rapids, Mich.: Eerdmans, 1971), 136.

5. Lesslie Newbigin, *Proper Confidence: Faith, Doubt and Certainty in Christian Discipleship* (Grand Rapids, Mich.: Eerdmans, 1995), 79–92: "Protestant fundamentalism is, like liberalism, a child of the Enlightenment. It has sought to reassert the authority of the Bible in the new situation created by modernity. The concern was right, but the method was wrong. I am referring to a kind of fundamentalism which seeks to affirm the factual, objective truth of every statement in the Bible and which thinks that if any single factual error were to be admitted, biblical authority would collapse" (85). Newbigin elaborates: "I have every sympathy with the fundamentalist's rejection of scholarship that denies any real authority to Scripture, but I cannot accept a kind of defense of the Bible that surrenders to the very forces threatening to destroy biblical authority" (86). N. T. Wright, in *Simply Christian: Why Christianity Makes Sense* (New York: HarperCollins, 2006), 183: "The rationalism of the Enlightenment infected even those who were battling against it."

6. Martin Buber, *I and Thou* (Eastford, Conn.: Martino Fine Books, 2010).

7. Holmes, *Faith Seeks Understanding*, 132.

8. Ibid., 150ff.

9. Ibid., 132.

10. Ibid.

11. Craddock, *As One without Authority*, 71.

12. Karl Barth, *Church Dogmatics*, III/3, ed. G. W. Bromiley and T. F. Torrance (Edinburgh: T. and T. Clark, 1961), 247.

13. John Calvin, *Institutes of the Christian Religion*, ed. John T. McNeill (Philadelphia: Westminster, 1960), I.8.13, 92.

14. Ibid.

15. N. T. Wright, *Simply Christian: Why Christianity Makes Sense* (New York: HarperCollins, 2006), 181.

16. Ibid., 183.

17. N. T. Wright has winsomely written in many places of this biblical theme of new creation. A very readable introduction is *Surprised by Hope: Rethinking Heaven, the Resurrection, and the Mission of the Church* (New York: HarperCollins, 2008).

18. Wright, *Simply Christian*, 184.

Chapter 17: All for a Letter

1. Stanley Grenz, *Theology for the Community of God* (Grand Rapids, Mich.: Eerdmans, 2000), 63–65. Grenz shows how the Trinity was neglected by most theologians over the last two centuries.

2. Cornelius Plantinga Jr., *Engaging God's World: A Christian Vision of Faith, Learning and Living* (Grand Rapids, Mich.: Eerdmans, 2002), 23.

3. Grenz, *Theology*, 71–74.

4. For an excellent overview of the multifaceted nature of human love reflecting the love within the Trinity, see Daniel Migliore, *Faith Seeking Understanding: An Introduction to Christian Theology*, 2nd ed. (Grand Rapids, Mich.: Eerdmans, 2004), 76–82.

5. Plantinga, *Engaging God's World*, 23.

6. Alister McGrath, *Understanding the Trinity* (Grand Rapids, Mich.: Zondervan, 1988), 148.

7. Leonardo Boff, *Trinity and Society* (Maryknoll, N.Y.: Orbis, 1988), 159.

8. *Eerdman's Handbook on the History of Christianity* (Grand Rapids, Mich.: Eerdmans, 1977), 158.

9. Diogenes Allen, *Philosophy for Understanding Theology* (Atlanta: John Knox Press, 1985), 106.

10. Timothy Keller, *The Reason for God: Belief in an Age of Skepticism* (New York: Dutton, 2008), 216.

11. Plantinga, *Engaging God's World*, 22.

12. Todd Hertz writes, "In his first movie since *Titanic*, James Cameron has made it worth the wait with a stunning milestone in filmmaking—and a storyline surprisingly rich in political and spiritual undertones." "Avatar," *Christianity Today*, December 17, 2009, *www.christianitytoday.com/ct/2009/decemberweb-only/avatar.html* (accessed March 9, 2015).

13. The definitive statement of this view is still considered to be that of Lynn White Jr., "The Historical Roots of Our Ecological Crisis," *Science* 155 (1967): 1203.

14. Migliore, *Faith Seeking Understanding*, 101.

15. Dallas Willard, *The Divine Conspiracy: Rediscovering Our Hidden Life in God* (New York: HarperCollins, 1998), 318.

Chapter 18: The Absurd

1. Hans Urs von Balthasar, *Elucidation*, trans. J. Riches (London: SPCK, 1975), 22.

2. John Macquarrie, *Thinking about God* (London: SCM Press, 1975), 41.

3. Paul Jewett, *God, Creation, and Revelation: A Neo-Evangelical Theology* (Eugene, Ore.: Wipf and Stock, 2000), 192.

4. Diogenes Allen, *Philosophy for Understanding Theology* (Atlanta: John Knox Press, 1985), 247.

5. Tony Campolo, *We Have Met Our Enemies and They Are Partly Right* (Waco: Word, 1985), 90ff.

6. Søren Kierkegaard, *Training in Christianity* (Princeton: Princeton Univ. Press, 1957), 123.

7. Robert E. Larsen, "Kierkegaard's Absolute Paradox," *Journal of Religion* 42 (January 1962): 34–43; Vernard Eller, "Fact, Faith, and Foolishness: Kierkegaard and the New Quest," *Journal of Religion* 48 (January 1968): 54–68.

8. Howard A. Johnston and Niels Thulstrup, eds., *A Kierkegaard Critique* (New York: Harper, 1962), 218.

9. Roger Hazelton, "The Nature of Christian Paradox," *Theology Today* 6 (October 1949), 57.

10. Recounted by, among others, Robert L. Perkins, *Søren Kierkegaard* (Atlanta: John Knox Press, 1969), 12.

11. Alan Richardson, *A Theological Word Book of the Bible* (New York: Macmillan, 1962), 198.

12. Quoted in Eller, "Fact, Faith, and Foolishness," 59.

13. Ibid.

14. Allen, *Philosophy for Understanding Theology*, 246.

15. Vernon Grounds, "The Nature of Faith," *Journal of the Evangelical Theological Society* (Fall 1963): 134: "Once faith has been exercised,

however, the absurd loses its irrationality and paradox ceases to be a heavy burden for the intellect to carry."

16. Allen, *Philosophy for Understanding Theology*, 245.

17. C. Stephen Evans, *Kierkegaard: An Introduction* (Cambridge: Cambridge Univ. Press, 2009), 9.

18. Cyril of Alexandria, quoted in Steven Boyer and Christopher Hall, *The Mystery of God: Theology for Knowing the Unknowable* (Grand Rapids, Mich.: Baker, 2012), 135. See pp. 131–34 for an overview of the heresies that shortchanged the divinity or humanity of Jesus.

19. Campolo, *We Have Met Our Enemies*, 88.

Chapter 19: The Shell

1. Oliver Wendell Holmes Sr., *The Autocrat of the Breakfast Table*, chapter 11, *http://en.wikiquote.org/wiki/Oliver_Wendell_Holmes,_Sr.#The_Autocrat_of_ the_Breakfast_Table_.281858.29* (accessed July 2014).

2. Daniel Migliore, *Faith Seeking Understanding: An Introduction to Christian Theology*, 2nd ed. (Grand Rapids, Mich.: Eerdmans, 2004), 6.

3. Ibid.

4. Ibid.

5. Cheryl Forbes, *Imagination: Embracing a Theology of Wonder* (Portland, Ore.: Multnomah, 1986), 165.

6. Eugene Peterson, *Under the Unpredictable Plant: An Exploration in Vocational Holiness* (Grand Rapids, Mich.: Eerdmans, 1992), 6.

7. George A. Lindbeck, "The Church's Mission to a Postmodern Culture," in *Postmodern Theology: Christian Faith in a Pluralist World*, ed. Frederick Burnham (San Francisco: Harper and Row, 1989), 41. Lindbeck cites literary critic Northrop Frye's conclusions in *The Great Code* for support of this position.

8. Ibid., 43.

9. Ibid.

10. Michael Macdonald and Andrew Tadie, eds., *G. K. Chesterton and C. S. Lewis: The Riddle of Joy* (London: Collins, 1989), 37.

11. Ibid., emphasis added.

12. Abraham Joshua Heschel, *God in Search of Man: A Philosophy of Judaism, Student's Guide* (New York: Farrar, Straus, Giroux, 1983), 34.

13. Michael Polyani, *The Tacit Dimension* (Chicago: Univ. of Chicago Press, 1966), 21–23. Lesslie Newbigin, in *Proper Confidence: Faith, Doubt, and Certainty in Christian Discipleship* (Grand Rapids, Mich.: Eerdmans, 1995), 40–64, offers a very readable introduction to Polyani and draws out many contemporary implications, especially Polyani's concept of personal knowledge.

14. Charles Kraft, *Christianity with Power* (Ann Arbor, Mich.: Servant, 1989). Kraft offers an excellent study of how worldviews are shaped by language.

15. David Robson, "There Really Are 50 Eskimo Words for 'Snow,'" *Washington Post*, www.washingtonpost.com/national/health-science/there -really-are-50-eskimo-words-for-snow/2013/01/14/e0e3f4e0–59a0–11e2 -beee-6e38f5215402_story.html (accessed February 2015).

16. Paul S. Fiddes, *Freedom and Limit: A Dialogue between Literature and Christian Doctrine* (Macon, Ga.: Mercer Univ. Press, 1999), 7.

17. Ibid.

18. M. Scott Peck, *The Road Less Travelled* (New York: Simon and Schuster, 1978), 32.

19. Antoine de Saint-Exupéry, www.goodreads.com/quotes/384067-if-you-want -to-build-a-ship-don-t-drum-up (accessed August 2015).

Chapter 20: If Not Certainty . . .

1. Os Guinness, *Doubt* (Tring, UK: Lion, 1976), 199.

2. Stanley Grenz, *Theology for the Community of God* (Grand Rapids, Mich.: Eerdmans, 2000), 408. Grenz speaks of three components of faith, recognized since the Reformation as *notitia* (knowledge), *assensus* (assent), and *fiducia* (trust). For my purposes, I did not consider *assensus*, or intellectual acknowledgment.

3. *The Constitution of the Presbyterian Church (USA), Part I, Book of Confessions* (Louisville: Office of the General Assembly, Presbyterian Church [USA], 2002), 31–32.

4. John H. Leith, *Basic Christian Doctrine* (Louisville: Westminster/John Knox Press, 1993), 174.

5. A. W. Tozer, *The Knowledge of the Holy* (San Francisco: Harper and Row, 1961), 1–2.

6. Ibid.

7. Pico Iyer, "The Folly of Thinking We Know," *New York Times* (March 20, 2014).

8. Ibid.

9. See Dave Goetz, "Reaching the Happy Thinking Pagan: A Conversation with Apologist Ravi Zacharias," *Leadership Journal* (Spring 1995): 18–27.

10. Reinhold Niebuhr, *The Nature and Destiny of Man*, vol. 1 (New York: Charles Scribner's Sons, 1941), 289.

11. Ibid.

12. Ibid., 331.

13. Lesslie Newbigin, *Proper Confidence: Faith, Doubt and Certainty in Christian Discipleship* (Grand Rapids, Mich.: Eerdmans, 1995), 66–67. I am indebted to Newbigin for the ideas in this paragraph on Enlightenment-inspired certainty versus biblical faith.

14. Eugene Peterson, *Tell It Slant: A Conversation on the Language of Jesus in His Stories and Prayers* (Grand Rapids, Mich.: Eerdmans, 2012), 116.

Chapter 21: Three Tensions

1. See Timothy Keller, *The Reason for God: Belief in an Age of Skepticism* (New York: Dutton, 2008), and William Lane Craig, *Reasonable Faith: Christian Truth and Apologetics* (Wheaton: Crossway, 2008).
2. Ronald Hepburn, *Christianity and Paradox: Critical Studies in Twentieth-Century Theology* (London: Watts and Co., 1958). I choose Hepburn as a conversation partner at this point because his book has been pivotal in this field, and he represents linguistic philosophy, often the Christian faith's most skeptical critic from a philosophical point of view.
3. Ibid., 16.
4. Ibid.
5. Ibid., 17. On the liberal side of this issue, see Gordon Graham, "Mystery or Mumbo-Jumbo?" *Philosophical Investigations* 7 (October 1984): 281–94; for a conservative view, see Vernon Grounds, "The Postulate of Paradox," *Bulletin of the Evangelical Theological Society* 7 (September 1974): 3–21.
6. Ibid., 22.
7. Ibid., 189.
8. C. S. Lewis, *Surprised by Joy* (New York: Harvest, 1984), 228.
9. Tertullian, *The Anti-Nicene Fathers*, vol. 3, *Latin Christianity: Its Founder, Tertullian* (Grand Rapids, Mich.: Eerdmans, 1963), 525. See also Bernard Williams, "Tertullian's Paradox," *New Essays in Philosophical Theology*, ed. Antony Flew and Alasdair Macintyre (New York: Macmillan, 1955), 190.
10. Gordon Graham, "Mystery or Mumbo-Jumbo?" *Philosophical Investigations* 7 (October 1984): 284ff.
11. Steven D. Boyer and Christopher A. Hall, *The Mystery of God: Theology for Knowing the Unknowable* (Grand Rapids, Mich.: Baker Academic, 2012), 161.
12. Graham, "Mystery or Mumbo-Jumbo?" 286.
13. Ibid., 288–89.
14. Boyer and Hall, *Mystery of God*, 161.
15. Anselm's *Prologion*, quoted in Geoffrey W. Bromiley, *Historical Theology: An Introduction* (Edinburgh: T. and T. Clark, 1978), 172.

Chapter 22: Simplicity and Complexity

1. Along with naive realism and critical realism, postmodernism is called "creative anti-realism," but this term seems overly complicated for this discussion. For a readable explanation of all three views, see David K. Naugle, *Worldview: The History of a Concept* (Grand Rapids, Mich.: Eerdmans, 2002), 321–25.

2. Thomas Kuhn, *The Structure of Scientific Revolutions*, 2nd ed. (Chicago: Chicago Univ. Press, 1970). See especially chapter 10, "Revolutions as Changes in Worldview."

3. T. F. Torrance, *Reality and Evangelical Theology* (Philadelphia: Westminster, 1982), 41.

4. Lesslie Newbigin, *Proper Confidence: Faith, Doubt and Certainty in Christian Discipleship* (Grand Rapids, Mich.: Eerdmans, 1995), 45–64. Newbigin offers a readable, concise overview of Polyani's work.

5. Paul Hiebert, *Missiological Implications of Epistemological Shifts: Affirming Truth in a Modern/Postmodern World* (Harrisburg, Pa.: Trinity Press, 1999), 69.

6. Naugle, *Worldview*, 322.

7. Parker Palmer, *The Promise of Paradox: A Celebration of Contradictions in the Christian Life* (San Francisco: Jossey-Bass, 1980), 2.

8. Ibid.

Chapter 23: Coastal Waters

1. C. S. Lewis, *The Abolition of Man* (New York: Macmillan, 1955), 88.

2. Ibid., 45.

3. Ibid., 34.

4. Diogenes Allen, *Philosophy for Understanding Theology* (Atlanta: John Knox Press, 1985), 58–59.

5. Ibid.

6. Gunther Bornkamm, "Mysterion," in Gerhard Kittle and Gerhard Friedrich, eds., *Theological Dictionary of the New Testament*, vol. 4 (Grand Rapids, Mich.: Eerdmans, 1977), 814.

7. Walter Bauer et al., *A Greek-English Lexicon of the New Testament and Other Early Christian Literature*, 2nd ed. (Chicago: Univ. of Chicago Press, 1979), 532.

8. Louis Bouyer, *The Christian Mystery* (Edinburgh: T. and T. Clark, 1989), 15.

9. Bornkamm, "Mysterion," 820.

10. Quoted in John Macquarrie, *Thinking about God* (London: SCM Press, 1975), 28.

11. Allen, *Philosophy for Understanding Theology*, 49.

12. Michael Foster, *Mystery and Philosophy* (London: SCM Press, 1957), 20.

13. Quoted in Macquarrie, *Thinking about God*, 32.

14. Ibid., 29. See also Allen, *Philosophy for Understanding Theology*, 265–70, who describes how Wittgenstein later changed his position.

15. Foster, *Mystery and Philosophy*, 46.

16. Richard J. Foster, *Prayer: Finding the Heart's True Home* (San Francisco: HarperCollins, 1992), 20.

17. Eugene Peterson, *Tell It Slant: A Conversation on the Language of Jesus in His Stories and Prayers* (Grand Rapids, Mich.: Eerdmans, 2012), 240. Peterson

makes his statement in relation to the mystery of the cross, but I believe it holds true for all Christian mystery.

18. Daniel Migliore, *Faith Seeking Understanding: An Introduction to Christian Theology*, 2nd ed. (Grand Rapids, Mich.: Eerdmans, 2004), 6.

19. Lesslie Newbigin, *Proper Confidence: Faith, Doubt and Certainty in Christian Discipleship* (Grand Rapids, Mich.: Eerdmans, 1995), 91.

20. Bornkamm, "Mysterion," 803.

21. Macquarrie, *Thinking about God*, 34.

22. George B. Hall, "D. M. Baillie: A Theology of Paradox," in *Christ, Church and Society: Essays on John Baillie and Donald Baillie*, ed. David A. S. Ferguson (Edinburgh: T. and T. Clark, 1993), 85.

Epilogue

1. L. Michael Ascher, "Therapeutic Paradox: A Primer," in *Therapeutic Paradox*, ed. L. Michael Ascher (New York: Guilford Press, 1989), 6.

2. Keith E. Webb, *The COACH Model for Christian Leaders* (Lexington, Ky.: Active Results, 2012), 72.

Afterword

1. *The Constitution of the Presbyterian Church (USA), Part I, Book of Confessions* (Louisville: Office of the General Assembly, Presbyterian Church [USA], 2002), 5.004.

2. D. M. Baillie, *God Was in Christ* (London: Faber, 1948), 114. See also George B. Hall, "D. M. Baillie: A Theology of Paradox," in *Christ, Church and Society: Essays on John Baillie and Donald Baillie*, ed. David A. S. Ferguson (Edinburgh: T. and T. Clark, 1993), 77.

3. Ibid., 82.

4. Walter Isaacson, "In Search of the Real Bill Gates," *Time* (January 13, 1997), 51.

5. John Jefferson Davis, *Foundations for Evangelical Theology* (Grand Rapids, Mich.: Baker, 1984), 125.

6. Eugene Peterson, *Tell It Slant: A Conversation on the Language of Jesus in His Stories and Prayers* (Grand Rapids, Mich.: Eerdmans, 2008), 150.

7. Dave Goetz, "Reaching the Happy Thinking Pagan," *Leadership Journal* (Spring 1995): 25.

8. Roger Hazelton, "The Nature of Christian Paradox," *Theology Today* 6 (October 1949): 44.